THE GREAT
BOOK OF TEXAS

The Crazy History of Texas with Amazing Random Facts & Trivia

A Trivia Nerds Guide
to the History of the
United States Vol.1

BILL O'NEILL

DON'T FORGET YOUR FREE BOOKS

<u>GET THEM FOR FREE ON
WWW.TRIVIABILL.COM</u>

CONTENTS

CHAPTER THREE:
TEXAS INVENTIONS, IDEAS, AND MORE!.......... 59

INTRODUCTION

How much do you really know about Texas?

Sure, you know that Texas is a state that's chock full of state pride. You know that it's an oil state and is home to the Dallas Cowboys. But what else do you *really* know about it?

By now, you've most likely heard about the Texas Revolution and the Battle of the Alamo. You probably know of Davy Crockett and you may have even heard that he died during the Battle of the Alamo, but do you know what really happened to him?

Have you ever wondered how Texas came to be known as the Lone Star State? Do you know who first discovered Texas? Do you know how many different flags have flown over Texas?

You've heard of Bush family legacy, but do you know which United States presidents were actually born in Texas?

Do you know about some of the paranormal folklore and unsolved mysteries of the state? Are you aware of odd sci-fi phenomenon that is believed to have occurred here?

If you have ever wondered about any of these things or more, then this book is for you! It's full of stories about Texas's history.

This isn't your typical book about Texas. It will guide you through some of the historical events and facts that have formed Texas into the incredible state it is today. You'll learn facts about the state that you may have never even wondered about. Once you've finished this book, you are going to know all there is to know about Texas.

Texas is a state that's rich in its history and culture. We will go all the way back to when the state was first founded and when it gained its independence from Mexico. We'll also jump forward to 2018 and take a closer look at some of the more recent historical icons whose roots were planted in Texas.

While this book will mostly follow a timeline of historical events, we will jump around some as we talk about Texas's history and other interesting facts about the state and the people who live in it.

This book is broken up into three easy-to-follow chapters to help you gain a better understanding of the Lone Star State. You'll learn some interesting facts about Texas that you'll be able to discuss with your friends or that may even make you want to visit this state!

Some of the facts you're about to learn are sad and some of them are shocking, but all of them are fascinating.

So, get ready to learn the following…

How did Texas get its name?

Why is it nicknamed the Lone Star State?

Who were the key players in the Battle of the Alamo?

Which *Disney* childhood stars came from Texas?

What sporting events got their start in Texas?

What animal did farmers and ranchers intentionally try to kill off?

And so much more!

CHAPTER ONE

TEXAS'S HISTORY AND RANDOM FACTS

Texas was the 28th state to enter the Union. The state is often represented by the Longhorn since it is the leading state in cattle production. But there's so much more to this state than its Longhorns. It's rich in both history and culture. Do you want to learn some interesting facts about Texas and its history? If so, then read on!

The Indians of Texas Gave the State Its Name

Before the Europeans settled in what is now known as Texas, the region was home to a number of different Native American tribes, now commonly known as the Indians of Texas. The area they occupied spanned from the Red River in Northern Texas to the Rio Grande in Southern Texas. Some of the major Native American tribes inhabiting Texas during this time included the Caddo, the Karankawa, the Coahuiltecan, the Lipan (Lipan-Apache), the Tonkawa, and the late-arriving Comanche.

Spanning across different regions of Texas, there was a world of cultural differences between these Native American tribes. Of all the Indians of Texas, the Caddo were the most well-developed tribe. They were known to be successful agriculturists.

It is from the Caddo that the state of Texas earned its name. Early Spanish authorities referred to a group within this tribe as the "Tejas," which was the Caddo's word for "friend." Texas was the Spanish pronunciation of the word Tejas.

The word "Tejano" also stemmed from the word "Teja." Tejano means a Mexican-American residing in Southern Texas.

The Last Battle of the Civil War Took Place in Texas

The last battle of the Civil War is highly controversial. Technically, the last major Civil War battle was the Battle of Appomattox Court, which took place in April 1865. During this battle, Confederate General Robert E. Lee surrendered.

However, most Americans recognize the Battle of Palmito Ranch as the last battle of the Civil War. It took place on May 12-13, 1865, in Brownsville, Texas. Although the Union and Confederates were already commencing upon a truce, Union Colonel Theodore H. Barrett ordered an attack, which took place near Fort Brown. It's been said that Barrett wanted to witness a battle before the war came to an end. The following day, the Confederacy retaliated and attacked near Palmito Ranch.

It may be surprising to some that the Confederates actually won this final battle, killing or wounding 30 Union soldiers. They also captured 100 other opponents. The Confederates were said to have been supplied by the French Army, which was occupying a nearby town in Mexico. Although it cannot be verified, it is also believed that the French Army provided the Confederates with a steam-powered gunboat that they used to patrol the Rio Grande.

The Confederates may have won the Battle of Palmito Ranch, but their victory didn't last too long. They officially surrendered and President Andrew Jackson ended the Union blockade of the Southern states in June of 1865.

Davy Crockett's Death Remains a Mystery

Legendary frontiersman and U.S. Congressman, David "Davy" Crockett, was one of the most famous people to fight in the Battle of the Alamo. He was a Congressman in Tennessee and had recently lost his seat. It's believed that he headed to Texas to help boost his political career, as his participation in the

Battle of the Alamo could have worked to his advantage.

When Davy Crockett arrived at the Alamo in early 1836, he was quickly identified as its leader. This was mostly due to his popularity, but the fact that he and his volunteers brought rifles with them helped to secure his position because the fort was poorly defended at the time of their arrival. His fame helped boost morale at the Alamo and he used his level-headed skillfulness in politics to help diffuse tensions that were occurring within the fort.

So, what exactly happened to Davy Crockett? Well, no one knows for sure. Davy Crockett was at the Alamo when the Mexican Army attacked on March 6, 1836. Most of the 200 men who were inside the fort perished during this attack, and although some of the soldiers surrendered, they were later killed. After the battle was over, it was rumored that Davy Crockett was one of them. However, other accounts at the time claimed that he was found dead inside the Alamo. To this day, Crockett's death remains a mystery.

Regardless of how Crockett died, word of his death spread all across Texas and the United States. Davy Crockett's participation in the battle was highly influential. Since he was such a famous person, it inspired others to come to continue to fight in the Battle of the Alamo.

Tejanos Fought in the Battle of the Alamo

Since the Battle of the Alamo was an attack instigated by the Mexican Army, it may be surprising for some to know that Tejanos fought as defenders in the battle.

Some historians regard the Tejanos who fought in the battle as the unsung heroes, as they often weren't idolized the same way Anglo-American defenders like Jim Bowie, Davy Crockett, and William Travis were. In fact, in many retellings of the Battle of the Alamo, the Tejanos' role was left out completely.

Before we discuss the battle, let's talk more about the Tejanos. The Tejanos who lived in San Antonio, which was then northeastern Mexico, lived apart from the rest of Mexico. They had formed a ranching community and a culture that was distinct from that of Mexico.

In 1821, Mexico gained its independence from Spain. During this time, Mexico welcomed U.S. settlers to inhabit Texas, which was under the control of the Mexican government. Most of the Tejanos recognized the financial benefits of immigrants and welcomed the U.S. settlers with open arms.

There's a bit of controversy among historians regarding what the objectives of the Tejanos really were. Some historians feel the Tejanos wanted their independence from Mexico and invited U.S. settlers to fight for their cause. Other historians think that the

Tejanos wanted Texas to have rights but they didn't want to actually break away from Mexico.

Regardless of their motivations, Tejanos played a critical role in Texas's independence. Some of the Tejanos who played a key role in the Battle of the Alamo included Juan Seguin, Gregorio Esparza, and José Toribio Losoya.

Six Flags Have Been Flown Over Texas

Have you ever heard the saying "six flags over Texas?" You may have seen the slogan at theme parks, shopping malls, and other places.

Maybe you have even heard that six flags have flown over Texas, but do you know the reason why?

Well, it all stems from 1519 when Spanish explorers first arrived in Texas. For a long time, the Spanish explorers had actually ignored Texas before their arrival in 1519. They didn't think there was anything in the area worth exploring.

It wasn't until the 1680s, when the Spanish found out that the French had established an outpost in Matagorda Bay, that the Spanish claimed ownership of Texas. The Spanish founded San Antonio in 1718.

In 1821, Mexico gained its independence from Spain and pushed them out of Texas. However, Texas did not remain under Mexico's control for very long after that.

In 1836, Texas became its own country, during which time it was called the Republic of Texas. Again, this didn't last too long. Texas agreed to become a part of the United States in 1845. But in 1861, it was one of 10 states that seceded to form the Confederacy. After the Civil War, Texas rejoined the Union in 1865, which it continues to remain a part of to this day!

As you've probably guessed by now, the six flags that have flown over Texas were from each of the countries that have ruled over the state.

The six flags that have flown over Texas are:

1. The flag of Spain (1519-1821)

2. The royal banner of France (1685-1690)

3. The flag of Mexico (1821-1836)

4. The flag of the Republic of Texas (1836-1845)

5. The flag of the United States of America (1845-1861 and 1865-present)

6. The flag of the Confederate States of America (1861-1865)

Many places throughout Texas continue to display the six flags today. However, some have removed the Confederate flag in recent years.

Why Texas is Nicknamed "The Lone Star State"

Have you ever wondered why Texas was nicknamed

the Lone Star State? It got the nickname from its flag. The Texas state flag, which was adopted when the state became the Republic of Texas, is called the Lone Star Flag. The reasoning for this is pretty simple: the flag has a single or "lone" white star.

The Lone Star Flag is made up of three colors: red, white, and blue. Each color on the flag embodies a different meaning. The red represents bravery, the white represents purity, and the blue represents loyalty.

There's also a meaning behind the lone star on the flag. The star is meant to represent "ALL of Texas and stands for our unity under God, State, and Country."

Many Texans still hang the Lone Star Flag as a reminder of Texas's independence.

Camels Were Once Brought to Texas

You might think that camels are only found in the Eastern hemisphere, zoos, or circuses, but this hasn't always been the case. In fact, at one point, camels were commonly seen in Texas!

In 1856, the United States Army began a program called the United States Camel Corps. Camels were brought in from countries such as Greece, Egypt, Turkey, and Malta. They were transported by boat to Indianola, Texas and were taken to Camp Verde.

Why would the U.S. Army bring camels to Texas? They wanted to experiment with using the camels as pack animals in the desert of Southwestern Texas.

In certain aspects, the camels did a great job in Texas. Not only did they fare well on a diet of prickly plants and scrubs, but the camels were also useful in areas where horses and mules weren't. They were able to go days at a time without water and even led soldiers to water holes, which saved lives.

As a whole, however, the United States Camel Corps experiment was largely unsuccessful. The camels didn't get along with the horses and mules. The horses and mules were so afraid of the camels that they would bolt. The camels were also difficult to handle and their odor was bothersome to the soldiers.

The U.S. Army stopped using camels in Texas during the Civil War after a failed attempt to carry mail between New Mexico and California.

So, what happened to those camels? While the government was able to round up 66 camels from the population, of which more than 100 had resided at Camp Verde and still more roamed the countryside, no one knows for sure what happened to those that remained uncaptured. The ones that were rounded up were sold off to circuses in the United States and Mexico in 1866.

But what about the camels that weren't rounded up? Well, they're a bit of a legend. It has been said that those camels may have continued to breed out in the wild. Some people even claim to see them today, but there are plenty of people who are skeptical about their existence. A camel sighting in Texas is often compared to a Chupacabra or Bigfoot sighting. If you happen to see a camel in Texas, just know that people might not believe your tale.

Sam Houston May Be Texas's Hero, But He Wasn't Even from Texas!

Sam Houston is by far the most well-known Texan in history. He has long been viewed as Texas's hero—and for good reason. Without him, Texas wouldn't be the state it is today. In fact, if it weren't for him, it wouldn't be a state *at all*.

After the deadly attack at the Alamo, Sam Houston and his troops caught the Mexican Army off-guard while they were sleeping on the banks of the San Jacinto River. Eight-hundred soldiers defeated the Mexican army, which was twice their size, in just 18 minutes. It was during the Battle of San Jacinto that Santa Anna surrendered and signed an armistice that gave Texas its independence.

Due to his heroism, it's not at all surprising that Sam Houston served as the first president of the Texas Republic. Eighty percent voted for him in the election.

He was later re-elected.

When Texas eventually became part of the United States again, Houston was elected as one of the state's senators.

Houston's heroism is memorialized in Texas in many ways. For starters, the city of Houston, which was the original capital of the state, was named after Sam Houston.

There's also a 67-foot statue of Sam Houston that stands in Huntsville, Texas. Though there are larger statues in the United States (including the Statue of Liberty and Our Lady of the Rockies), the Sam Houston statue is the largest statue in America that's modeled after a real person.

The kicker to all of this? Though he may be Texas's hero, Sam Houston wasn't even *from* Texas! Houston was born in Rockbridge County, Virginia.

He later started his political career in Tennessee, where he was elected Governor. He resigned from office after his wife Eliza left him and made his infidelity and alcoholism public knowledge. He then went to live with a Cherokee tribe in Arkansas, where he became an honorary Cherokee and married a Cherokee woman.

Thirty years after resigning from his position as Governor of Tennessee, he was elected Governor of

Texas (making him the only Governor to have ever been elected to serve in that capacity for two states).

Regardless of where he was born, Sam Houston was a pretty remarkable guy!

The Texas State Capital Was Named After "The Father of Texas"

While Houston was named after Sam Houston, the new capital of Texas was named after another important figure in Texas history. Austin, Texas, was named after Stephen F. Austin, "The Father of Texas."

So, who was the man that gave Texas's capital city its name? Why was he important?

Stephen F. Austin was the first to establish an Anglo-American colony in Texas when it was a province of Mexico. During his time, Texas grew into an independent republic.

The idea wasn't actually Stephen F. Austin's. It was his father, Moses Austin, who was the first to take steps towards establishing a colony in the region. Moses Austin traveled to San Antonio with a petition that would grant him land and received permission to establish a settlement of 300 families across 200,000 acres of land. However, Moses Austin died before he was able to accomplish his plans, leaving Stephen F. Austin to complete the settlement.

Stephen F. Austin was responsible for more than just

establishing the settlement. He also oversaw immigration, established a law enforcement system, allocated land, and ensured the development of social infrastructure (e.g. roads, sawmills).

Without Stephen F. Austin, Texas wouldn't be what it is today.

There Was Once a Death at the Texas State Fair

The Texas State Fair is the largest fair in the United States. Although the fair doesn't formally document the number of attendees, it's estimated that about 3 million people visit the fair every year.

The Texas State Fair is most well-known for its 55-foot statue and greeter, Big Tex, the world's tallest cowboy. It also has the largest Ferris wheel in the entire Western Hemisphere! Some of the foods you'll find include corn dogs, Frito pies, and turkey legs. There's live entertainment, exhibits, and other fun attractions. It's one experience you won't want to miss out on.

But not every day has gone smoothly at the Texas State Fair. In 1979, there was an accident involving the Swiss Skyride gondola cars. One of the gondola cars got caught on a tower. A second car ended up crashing into it, which caused both cars to plummet 85 feet into the tent-covered game booths below.

The accident is one that never should have happened

at all. It was caused by 90 mph winds.

91-year-old Fred Millard, who was a passenger in the first gondola car, died. His wife and young daughters were among 17 people injured in the accident. One woman was left paralyzed as a result of the accident. She died in 1986.

About $10 million was awarded to victims of the accident in court settlements.

The Swiss Skyride was immediately shut down following the incident. The ride has since been replaced, however. In 2007, a new and improved Texas Skyway gondola ride could be found at the fair. The new gondola ride has better safety features to prevent another accident from occurring.

You Can Watch a Movie Where Lee Harvey Oswald Was Arrested

Lee Harvey Oswald, who assassinated the late President John F. Kennedy, was arrested at the Texas Theater in Dallas, Texas.

What some may not know is that Lee Harvey Oswald wasn't originally arrested for killing the president. He was first arrested for shooting and killing Dallas police officer J. D. Tippit.

Oswald's arrest came about on November 22, 1963, when a shoe store manager named John Brewer noticed him loitering suspiciously outside his store.

Brewer noted that Oswald fit the description of the suspect in the shooting of Officer Tippit. When Oswald continued up the street and slipped inside the Texas Theater without paying for a ticket, Brewer called a theater worker, who alerted authorities.

Fifteen Dallas police officers arrived at the scene. When they turned on the movie house lights, they found Lee Harvey Oswald sitting towards the back of the theater. The movie that had been airing at the time was *War is Hell.*

When Lee Harvey Oswald was questioned by authorities about Tippit's homicide, Captain J. W. Fritz recognized his name as one of the workers from the book depository who had been reported missing and was already being considered a suspect in JFK's assassination. The day after he was formally arraigned for murdering Officer Tippit, he was also charged with assassinating John F. Kennedy.

Today, the Texas Theater is a historical landmark that is commonly visited by tourists. It still airs movies and hosts special events. There's also a bar and lounge.

The Texas Theater was the first theater in Texas to have air conditioning. It was briefly owned by famous aviator and film producer, Howard Hughes.

Texas's Capitol Building is the Largest in the United States *and* It's Haunted

One might think that the largest Capitol building in the country is the nation's Capitol in Washington, D.C., but you'd be wrong. In fact, the Texas State Capitol stands seven feet higher than the nation's capitol building. It's the largest state Capitol in the United States!

Located in Austin, Texas, the Texas State Capitol was one of the top seven tallest buildings in the world when it was built. Built of limestone and granite, Texas's Capitol building has a statue of a lady with a sword on top. The 16-foot, 2,000-pound aluminum Goddess of Liberty statue sits on top of the Capitol building.

Aside from its size, there's also something else pretty well-known (and dare we say cool?) about the Texas State Capitol building. It's haunted. There have been numerous reports of ghost sightings in the Capitol building. Visitors have claimed to have had encounters with the ghosts of Sam Houston, Andrew Hamilton, and Edmond Jackson Davis. Some have even claimed to see the ghost of a "lady in red."

Bonnie and Clyde Are Buried in Texas

Surely, you've heard the story of Bonnie and Clyde, love-struck lovers and partners in crime. They're probably the most infamous outlaws of all time. There's no doubt this iconic couple has gone down in history. There have been movies made and songs written about them. But did you know that Bonnie and Clyde had roots in Texas?

Both Bonnie and Clyde were born in Texas. Clyde Barrow was born in Ellis County, Texas, in 1909. The following year, Bonnie Parker was born in Abilene, Texas.

Their story begins in West Dallas where the two met in 1930 at a mutual friend's house. Clyde had been caring for the friend, who had a broken arm, when Bonnie stopped by. At the time, Bonnie was just 19 years old and married to a man who was in jail. She remained married to him until the day she died. In fact, it's even been said that she died wearing her wedding ring.

Upon meeting, Bonnie and Clyde were instantly taken with one another. It was love at first sight. Many historians believe that the entire reason Bonnie remained by Clyde's side through their violent crime spree was because she loved him.

When she took Clyde to her mother's home to meet her mom, he was arrested for a robbery he had committed in Waco. When she visited him in jail, she smuggled in a gun that would help him escape. She hoped that Clyde would get on the straight and narrow, but instead she ended up joining him on his crime sprees.

The outlaws traveled the United States in stolen cars and committed both robberies and murders together. They received national attention when they robbed a National Guard armory, killing nine policemen and stealing an arsenal of weapons. The FBI and other law enforcement officers began to chase them.

In May of 1934, Bonnie and Clyde were killed in Bienville Parish, Louisiana. They were shot by four Texas officers and two Louisiana officers.

While Bonnie and Clyde are both buried in Dallas, Texas, their bodies are interred at two different cemeteries. Clyde is buried in a family plot with his brother, Marvin "Buck" Barrow, at Western Heights Cemetery. Bonnie is buried at Crown Memorial Park.

Want to spend the night where Bonnie and Clyde rested? If so, then one Texas landmark you may want to check out is the Fort Worth's Stockyards Hotel, which the partners in crime used as a hideout. The room they stayed in is called "The Bonnie & Clyde Suite." It has a number of historic artifacts, including a poem Bonnie wrote for Clyde and her .38 revolver.

Two United States Presidents Were Born in Texas

Did you know that two United States presidents were born in Texas? What you might be surprised to learn is that they weren't George W. Bush or George H. W. Bush! Though the Bushes are well-known for establishing their political careers in Texas, both father and son were born in New England states.

So, which presidents *were* born in Texas?

Dwight Eisenhower was born in Denison, Texas, though he moved to Kansas when he was just a toddler. He later became the 34th President of the United States.

Lyndon B. Johnson, however, had strong roots in Texas. His family founded Johnson City, and he was born in nearby Stonewall, Texas. Johnson was a U.S. representative and later a U.S. senator in Texas before becoming the Vice President of the United States.

Ironically, Johnson became the President of the United States while he was in his home state. You see, Lyndon B. Johnson wasn't actually elected to be the President. He was John F. Kennedy's Vice President. It wasn't until John F. Kennedy was assassinated in Dallas by Lee Harvey Oswald on November 22, 1963, that Johnson became president.

Just two hours after JFK was assassinated, Lyndon B.

Johnson was sworn into office aboard Air Force One while it was stationed at Dallas Love Field Airport.

A Popular Card Game Has Texas Origins

As its name suggests, Texas Hold'em was started in the Lone Star State. While it's unknown who exactly came up with the idea of Texas Hold'em, the game can be traced back to Robstown, Texas, in the early 1900s.

The game began to spread like wildfire throughout Texas. In 1967, a group of Texan card players took the game to Las Vegas. One of those card players was Crandell Addington, who is one of the co-founders of the World Series of Poker. Addington is also a member of the Poker Hall of Fame.

The game was originally called Hold'em before it was taken to Vegas. It was there that it received the name Texas Hold'em.

The Golden Nugget in Las Vegas was the first and only casino to offer Texas Hold'em. Unfortunately, the casino's poker room didn't receive many high-paying players. As a result, the game didn't become popular. It wasn't until top poker players were invited to play Hold'em at the Dunes Casino that it gained popularity with gamblers.

In 1969, Texas Hold'em was added to the Second Annual Gambling Fraternity Convention. The following year, this convention was renamed the World Series of Poker. No-limit Hold'em became the main event, and has remained the main event ever since.

Today, Texas Hold'em is one of the most popular types of poker.

RANDOM FACTS

1. The Alamo is Texas's most popular historic site. It gets more than 2 million visitors every year who come to see the buildings, which have been restored, and the monument honoring all of the fallen soldiers.

2. In 1836, Sam Houston defeated Stephen F. Austin in the presidential election. However, Austin was appointed as Secretary of State, a position that he held until he died later that year.

3. Sam Houston wasn't happy about Austin's location as capital. He believed that it was too remote, which would make it difficult to defend from the Mexican Army and the Native Americans.

4. Despite being a slave owner himself, Sam Houston was actually against slavery. He voted against making slavery more widespread in the United States and refused to swear allegiance to the Confederate States of America. This led to him being removed from his position as Governor of Texas.

5. Texas is unique in terms of how it came to be a part of the United States. It's the only state that

did not become a part of the country by territorial annexation. Instead, it became a part of the United States by treaty. It took years of debate before it happened. The issue that caused the debate was slavery. Texas had a large population of slaves, with 30,000 of its 125,000 residents being slaves. People throughout the United States feared that adding a new slave state would interfere with Congress and other political issues.

6. Each year on March 2nd, Texans celebrate Texas Independence Day. It commemorates the state gaining its independence from Mexico. The day is also known as Texas Flag Day and Sam Houston Day. To celebrate the state's independence, there are festivals which include live band performances, chili cook-offs, re-enactments, and more.

7. Six Flags amusement park, which was founded in 1961, was named after Texas's six flags! Though there are several locations throughout the country, the original park is located in Arlington, Texas. It is split into several different sections, with park attractions depicting the six flags that have flown over Texas, including Spanish and Mexican sections of the park.

8. There's a popular myth that Texas could secede from the United States of America at any time. This isn't true. However, the state of Texas *could*

hypothetically change in the future. In Texas's 1845 annexation agreement, it was decided that the state could divide into five different states without approval of the U.S. government. Although no attempts have actually been made to divide Texas into five states, state lawmakers have toyed with the idea of dividing Texas into two states.

9. Texas has the highest maximum highway speed limit in all of America. There's a stretch of highway between Austin and San Antonio that allows you to drive at 85 mph. If you love to speed, then you just might love Texas.

10. Three of the top ten most populated cities in the United States are located in Texas. These cities include Houston (population of 2.3 million), San Antonio (of 1.49 million), and Dallas (of 1.3 million).

11. The Texas Rangers are the oldest statewide law enforcement agency in the United States. The force came into existence in 1823. The Texas Ranger Hall of Fame museum is located in Waco. Members of the Texas Rangers included Will Rogers, John Wayne, Chuck Norris, and former President George H. W. Bush.

12. As the saying goes, "Everything is bigger in Texas." Well, Texas itself is pretty big. It's the

second-largest state in the United States. The first-largest state is Alaska and the third-largest state is California. Encompassing 268,820 square miles, the state of Texas is two times the size of Germany!

13. Although you might think the saying "Don't mess with Texas" came about because of its state pride, it actually originated as a part of its anti-litter campaign. The state spent about $20 million annually to clean up trash along its highways. The slogan was designed to help with its anti-litter campaign. It gained so much popularity that Texans display it on bumper stickers, shirts, and anywhere else they want to show off their state pride today.

14. Like most states, there are still a number of odd laws perpetuated in Texas. It's illegal to sell your eye, milk another person's cow, take more than three sips of beer while standing, or shoot a buffalo from the second story of a hotel.

15. Texas has its own Eiffel Tower. The 65-foot tower was built in Paris, Texas, in 1995. It has been boasted as the "second-largest Eiffel Tower in the second-largest Paris."

16. There are more than 145 languages spoken in Texas. Aside from English, you'll hear everything from German and Vietnamese to Hindu and

Tagalog spoken in this state!

17. Texas's state motto is "friendship." It was chosen due to the Caddo's meaning of the word Tejas.

18. Though Texas is a part of the United States, the state still owns all of its public lands. What does this mean? In order for the United States to build anything within the borders of Texas, it must first ask for permission. This includes public or state parks.

19. The Lone Star State has sued the United States more than 40 times in the past 100 years over everything from women's health to the environment. Most of those lawsuits occurred during the Obama Administration.

20. As of 2010, Texas had a population of more than 25.1 million people.

Test Yourself – Questions and Answers

1. What does the word Tejas mean?

    a. Friends
    b. Enemies
    c. Soldiers

2. Which United States President *wasn't* born in Texas?

    a. Lyndon B. Johnson
    b. George W. Bush
    c. Dwight Eisenhower

3. Why is Texas known as the Lone Star State? What was it nicknamed after?

    a. The country band called Lonestar
    b. A horse named Lone Star who won a lot of races in Texas
    c. The Lone Star flag of the Texas Republic

4. Who was the first President of the Texas Republic?

    a. Davy Crockett
    b. Lyndon B. Johnson
    c. Sam Houston

5. Which animal was brought to Texas in the 1850s by the United States Army to help assist soldiers traveling in the desert?

    a. Camels
    b. Kangaroos
    c. Mules

Answers

1. a.
2. b.
3. c.
4. c.
5. a.

CHAPTER TWO

TEXAS'S POP CULTURE

Texas is a state that's rich in pop culture. It's had a huge influence on one genre of music, in particular. Do you know which one? Do you know which famous Tejano singer has roots in Texas or where she's buried? Have you heard about the influential musician who was bullied while she was growing up in Texas? To discover the answers to these and other interesting facts, read on!

Country Music Started Out in Texas

Country music is the most listened to genre of music on radio stations today. Have you ever wondered how country music came to be?

Well, it all started back in the early 1900s with a Texas fiddler named Eck Robertson. Robertson grew up on a farm and started learning how to play the fiddle at the age of five. He later learned to play the banjo and guitar.

In 1904, a sixteen-year-old Robertson decided that he wanted to become a professional musician and began to travel and play his music. Two years later, Eck Robertson met his wife. Together, they performed at fiddling contests and silent-movie theaters.

Eck Robertson later met 74-year-old fiddler, Henry C. Gilliland. In 1922, the two traveled to New York City where they auditioned for and secured a recording contract with the Victor Talking Machine Company. They recorded the first four country songs every produced, but only two of them—"Turkey in the Straw" and "Arkansas Traveler"—ended up being released. Robertson was asked to return to the studio to record six more songs, this time without Gilliland.

Country music has come a long way since then, but we can thank Texas for its beginnings.

And the First Country Album to Go Platinum Came from Texan Musicians!

The first country album to go platinum was a collaboration of more than one artist. The album was called *Wanted! The Outlaws* and featured songs from Texas natives Waylon Jennings and Willie Nelson. It also featured Jessi Colter (Waylon Jennings's wife) and Thomas Paul "Tompall" Glaser.

The album, which was released in 1976 by RCA Records, was inclusive of songs that had already been released. It was the record label's attempt at getting music performed by Waylon Jennings to sell, as well as marketing music by Willie Nelson, who was outselling Jennings.

RCA Records also hoped to capitalize on outlaw country music, which was a new subgenre of country music. Outlaw was considered to be more progressive in terms of sound and emphasized the drug culture.

The country album was the first in history to gain platinum status when it reached one million sales.

Wanted! The Outlaws quickly rose to the top of country charts, hitting number one, and also earned a #10 spot on the pop charts.

Two hit singles came from the album. They were "Suspicious Minds" and "Good Hearted Woman."

The Richest Female Musician is From Texas, But She's Not a Country Singer

As of 2017, R&B/Pop singer Beyoncé Knowles-Carter was the highest-paid female musician by a landslide. That year alone, she made $105 million! Many may not know that Queen Bey was born and raised in Houston, Texas.

Beyoncé and Solange Knowles are often considered Texas's most famous sisters.

Beyoncé first began competing in the local talent shows. The singer says she sold her very first song at St. John's United Methodist Church in Houston.

In 2017, Beyoncé went back to her home state to help with Hurricane Harvey relief efforts. She, her mother Tina Knowles, and her former band member Michelle Williams all went to Houston to help distribute supplies to those in need. They handed out food and diapers to Hurricane Harvey victims. Through her organization BeyGOOD, the singer also donated cots, wheelchairs, feminine products, and more to those in need.

This wasn't the first time Beyoncé has made charitable contributions to her hometown. In 2017, she donated $7 million to help with Houston's homeless.

Although she's not a country singer, Beyoncé has mentioned that she wants to make a country music album at one point. Though she has yet to release a full country album, the singer *did* record a country track called "Daddy Lessons" for her *Lemonade* album. The song has received support from a number of artists within the country music community, including Dierks Bentley and Karen Fairchild from Little Big Town. It should be interesting to see if Beyoncé will revisit her country roots in her music in the future.

This Famous Singer Was Bullied While She Was Growing Up in Texas

Janis Joplin is often considered one of the most influential musicians of all-time. Countless singers have credited her influence over their own music. But did you know that Janis Joplin wasn't always that popular? In fact, she was bullied in Texas.

Growing up in Port Arthur, Texas, Janis Joplin was an excellent student with a bright future. She was involved in extracurricular activities in high school, such as Glee Club and the Future Teachers of America. But high school wasn't all rainbows and butterflies for Joplin.

Janis Joplin was bullied by former NFL coach Jimmy Johnson, with whom she went to high school. This led Joplin to become the rebel of the small town she grew up in. She colored her hair and spent a lot of time in blues bars.

After high school, Joplin headed off to Texas University. Unfortunately, college wasn't any better for her when it came to bullying. In fact, she dropped out after just one semester because the other students were so mean to her. She was voted "The Ugliest Man on Campus" by the Texas University fraternities. Though the singer went on to have great success, that label was said to have haunted her for the rest of her short life.

You Can Celebrate Selena's Life in Corpus Christi

By now, you've probably already heard of Grammy-winning Tejano musician Selena Quintanilla-Perez, who was murdered at a hotel in Corpus Christi, Texas. Today, she's considered a legend.

For those who don't already know the story, it goes like this: Selena, who was considered the Queen of the Tejano world, was just 23 years old when she was murdered on March 31, 1995. At the time of her death, Selena's fame had been on the rise. Between United States and international sales, she and her family, who performed her backup music, had sold more than 60 million albums. She was most well-known for her songs "Como la Flor", "Bidi Bidi Bom Bom", and "Dreaming of You."

Her life came to a tragic end after she confronted her friend and fan club president, Yolanda Saldivar, about stolen documents at a Days Inn in Corpus Christi. The documents would prove that Saldivar was stealing money from Selena. Saldivar refused to provide her with the documents. She told Selena that she had been raped. Selena drove her to the hospital, where doctors said Saldivar had been lying.

When Selena and Yolanda Saldivar returned to the hotel, they argued. Saldivar shot Selena in the back when she turned to leave the hotel room. Selena ran to the hotel lobby for help. She named Saldivar as the person who had shot her before she fell to the floor. Selena was pronounced dead upon arrival to the hospital.

Saldivar had gone to her car and pointed a gun at her own head as she was surrounded by police officers before surrendering.

Selena had become a household name throughout much of the world, but people in her home state really loved her. On the day of her death, Texas radio and television stations received many calls from distraught fans and listeners.

Yolanda Saldivar was sentenced to life in prison without the likelihood of being granted parole. Although a rumor starts every few years that Saldivar has died, it has been confirmed that she remains alive in the Mountain View Correctional Unit in Gatesville, Texas.

There was a movie called *Selena*, which starred Jennifer Lopez, about the life and death of the Tejano musician. The movie made $35 million at the box office and helped Lopez rise to fame.

Selena's legacy is still kept alive in Corpus Christi today. There are a number of ways you can celebrate the life of the Tejano singer when you're visiting the city.

For starters, there's a Selena Museum that was started by the musician's family. It's in the old music studio where the family used to create their records. You'll get a tour of the studio room, which was the same one used in the movie *Selena*. Other things you'll see at the museum include some of her iconic outfits, her Grammy award, her red Porsche, her decorative egg collection, a display of Selena Barbie dolls, and so much more. The museum is every Selena fan's dream.

There's also a memorial statue called the Mirador de la Flor, or Selena's Seawall. The monument is located at the corner of Shoreline Boulevard and Peoples Street T-Head. Hundreds of fans visit her memorial every week.

Selena is buried at Seaside Memorial Park in Corpus Christi. Some people believe that the gravesite may even be haunted by Selena's ghost! There have been reports of hearing the late musician singing near her grave. Some have even claimed to see what they believe to be the ghost of Selena walking along the Seawall.

Eeyore's Birthday is Celebrated in Austin

Are you a fan of *Winnie-the-Pooh*? If so, you might want to visit Austin, Texas, to celebrate Eeyore's birthday. Yes, that's right. The city celebrates the fictional donkey's birthday in the form of a festival, which usually takes place on the last Saturday of April at Pease Park.

This festival began in 1963 when the English Department students at the University of Texas at Austin chose the theme for their spring picnic. The reason they chose Eeyore's birthday as the theme for the picnic was that in A. A. Milne's *Winnie-the-Pooh* stories, Eeyore thinks his friends Winnie, Tigger, Piglet, Owl, and Rabbit have forgotten his birthday, when in reality they had planned a surprise birthday party for him.

The very first year of the party, the students had a picnic. They brought honey (because what would a *Winnie-the-Pooh* themed picnic be without some honey?), lemonade, beer, a maypole, and a live donkey draped in flowers.

The theme of the picnic was embraced by Austin's hippie community. Today, that Eeyore themed picnic has evolved into a huge festival. It's still celebrated by much of the hippie community, as well as the hipsters. Many of the original college alumni still attend the event with their families.

Sponsored by the Friends of the Forest Foundation, Eeyore's Birthday Party in Austin has a number of festivities. You'll find live music, food and drink vendors, and more. Proceeds go to support local charities.

The party begins at 11 a.m. and runs until dusk. There are typically costumes and costume contests, so don't be afraid to dress up. However, clothes tend to come off later at night, so parents with children might consider attending the festival earlier in the day.

To keep the spirit of Eeyore's birthday going, there's always a maypole and a live donkey in attendance at the festival every year!

Three *Disney* Child Stars Were Born in Texas

If you're a fan of *Disney*, it might surprise you to know that three of your favorite child actresses came from Texas.

Lizzie McGuire actress Hilary Duff and her older sister Haylie Duff both grew up in Texas. Their father owns a chain of Texas convenience stores, so Hilary grew up between Houston and San Antonio, where the stores are located.

The Duffs' mother encouraged both girls to pursue acting, singing, and ballet. They both performed at local theaters, as well as appearing in a San Antonio theater's production of *The Nutcracker*.

Hilary Duff's mom moved her and her sister to California in 1993 to pursue their acting careers. Hilary earned a few small roles before being cast in her first major film, *Casper Meets Wendy*.

In 2001, the *Lizzie McGuire* show premiered. Hilary Duff became a household name. She gained even more attention that year when media caught wind of her relationship with pop singer Aaron Carter.

Another *Disney* actress who started out in Texas? Selena Gomez! The actress was born in Grand Prairie, Texas. Selena Gomez's mother was also a former stage actress. Selena became interested in an acting career while watching her mother prepare for the stage. Her first role was in *Barney & Friends*, which is where she first met our third Texan who went on to become a *Disney* star—Demi Lovato.

Despite being born in Albuquerque, New Mexico, "Sorry Not Sorry" singer Demi Lovato grew up in Dallas. The star's mother was a former Dallas Cowboys Cheerleader. Lovato has credited her mother's stories about the difficulty of being a Dallas Cowboys Cheerleader, with teaching her the value of hard work.

Demi Lovato also has a half-sister named Madison Lee De La Garza, who played fellow Texan Eva Longoria's daughter in the show *Desperate Housewives*.

Barney & Friends Was Filmed in Dallas

Barney, the purple dinosaur, was an iconic character for millennial children. Did you know that *Barney & Friends* got its start in Dallas, TX?

The concept of the series was created by Dallas native Sheryl Leach, a former inner-city school teacher and marketing executive. Leach thought there was a market for preschool-aged children. She couldn't have been more accurate. The series had a seventeen-year run! It initially aired on PBS Kids in April of 1992 until production stopped in September of 2009.

During the time it aired, the series was filmed in the Dallas area. It makes sense why Selena Gomez and Demi Lovato were part of the cast of *Barney & Friends*.

The series might make a comeback. A series revival was initially discussed for 2017, but there hasn't been any word yet on when or if *Barney & Friends* is still set to return. We hope if it does return, it will still be filmed in Dallas.

Lots of Movies Have Been Filmed in Texas

Quite a few movies have been filmed in Texas. This is partly due to the nice weather, but it's also because the NASA Johnson Space Center is a popular filming location for many sci-fi movies.

Here's a list of a few of the many movies that have had scenes filmed in the Lone Star State:

- *Miss Congeniality*, starring Sandra Bullock, features some scenes that were filmed in San Antonio and Austin. There were scenes filmed on Congress Street in Austin and at two Austin hotels, the Driskill Hotel and the Hyatt Downtown.

- *Pearl Harbor* was filmed in Corpus Christi. A large part of the movie was filmed aboard the USS Lexington in the Corpus Christi Bay. The film stars Ben Affleck, Josh Hartnett, Alec Baldwin, and Cuba Gooding, Jr. Filming the movie on the USS Lexington proved to be controversial, with war veterans being infuriated over the ship being used to portray a Japanese ship.

- *What's Eating Gilbert Grape*, featuring Johnny Depp and Leonardo DiCaprio, was filmed in Manor, Texas. Gilbert works at a grocery store set in a fictional town in the movie. The actual grocery store in the film was Manor Grocery.

- *Armageddon* features scenes that were filmed at the Johnson Space Center. There were also scenes filmed in Denton, TX.

- *Transformers: Dark of the Moon* contains a scene that was shot at the Johnson Space Center.

- *Boyhood* was filmed in and around Houston. Some of the scenes were filmed on location at Minute Maid Park and the Houston Museum of Natural Science.

- *Terms of Endearment,* starring Shirley MacLaine and Jack Nicholson, features scenes that were shot throughout the Houston area. In the movie, the couple's lunch scene was filmed at Brennan's Restaurant in Midtown Houston. Scenes were also filmed on location at East Beach, Leon's Gourmet Grocer, the University of Nebraska, Lincoln General Hospital, and Lincoln Municipal Airport.

- *Space Cowboys,* starring Clint Eastwood, contains scenes that were filmed at the Johnson Space Center.

- *Apollo 13* is another movie that was filmed at the Johnson Space Center.

- *Any Given Sunday* contains scenes that were filmed at the Texas Stadium.

- *Boys Don't Cry,* starring Hilary Swank, was filmed in Texas, even though the actual story that the movie is based on took place in Nebraska. Scenes were filmed on location at Dad's Broadway Skateland in Mesquite, the Hunt County Courthouse in Greenville, and the McKinney Grain Company in McKinney. Scenes were also filmed throughout Crandall, Texas.

Other movies that were filmed in Texas include *The Rookie, The Tree of Life,* and *Any Given Sunday.*

A *Supernatural* Star Owns a Brewery in the Austin Area

Best known for his role as Dean Winchester in the hit show *Supernatural*, Jensen Ackles was born in Dallas, Texas.

Though he moved to Los Angeles to pursue acting, Ackles recently moved back to Texas with his wife and child.

Jensen Ackles and his brother-in-law recently decided to turn their hobby of brewing beer into a business. On January 10th, 2018, their craft brewery, Family Business Beer Co., opened in the Austin area.

It's unlikely that you'll actually see Ackles working at the brewery since he spends most of the year filming *Supernatural* in Vancouver, B.C. But hey, you never know!

The actor told KXAN-TV that you might also be able to spot him at ABGB, his favorite brewpub in Austin.

Ackles' friend and *Supernatural* co-star Jared Padalecki, who plays his brother Sam Winchester, also lives in the Austin area.

Late Actor Patrick Swayze Fell in Love with Horses in Texas

Though you might think he only had a love for dancing, *Dirty Dancing* actor Patrick Swayze also loved horses.

Swayze, who is also well-known for his role in the movie *Ghost*, was born and raised in Houston, Texas. The actor, who lived in the Oak Forest community of Houston until he was 20, was quite the equestrian. He even learned calf-roping!

His love of horses first began when he was a young boy. He visited Gleannloch Farms during this time, which is where he first fell in love with Arabian horses. He saw their horse named Morafic, which he later credited for the reason he fell in love with the Arabian breed.

You might be wondering how Swayze got into dancing when his horses were his real passion. His love for dance came from his mom, Patsy Swayze. She was a dancer herself, as well as a dance instructor and film choreographer. Patsy Swayze later choreographed movies such as *Urban Cowboy* and *Hope Floats*.

Patsy Swayze founded the Houston Jazz, of which she was the director. She also later opened the Swayze School of Dance, where Patrick was one of her students. It was there that he met the woman he would later go on to marry, Lisa Niemi, who also had a love for acting and was a fellow horse fanatic.

After his rise to fame, Patrick Swayze took a break from show business in order to breed Arabian horses with his wife. Due to their acting schedules, most of their horse shows were in Texas. They personally competed in the Dallas/Fort Worth big region IX show.

Patrick Swayze's favorite horse was a chestnut Arabian stallion named Tamsen.

Prior to losing his battle with pancreatic cancer in 2009, Swayze chose to live out his final months of life at his horse ranch with his wife. One of their stallions attended his memorial service.

A *Gossip Girl* Actress Was Born While Her Parents Were in Prison in Texas

Gossip Girl and *Roommate* actress Leighton Meester was born in Texas while both of her parents were in prison. Leighton's parents, along with her aunt and grandfather on her mom's side, were arrested for smuggling 1,200-pound marijuana shipments out of Jamaica.

Though it was originally rumored that Leighton was born in prison, she was born in a hospital. Leighton's mom had to serve 16 months in prison after she was born.

News of the story broke when *US Weekly* released an article about it. The cover read "She overcame!" And we would have to agree. Leighton's story is very inspiring. Despite her family's difficult past, the actress was still able to land her role as Blair Waldorf on *Gossip Girl* and become a household name.

Late Actress Debbie Reynolds Loved Growing Up in El Paso, But She Didn't Visit Often

Late actress Debbie Reynolds, who was famous for starring in films like *Singin' in the Rain, Tammy and the Bachelor*, and *Halloweentown*, said her El Paso upbringing helped shape her career in Hollywood.

The actress grew up in El Paso during the Great Depression. During that time, she would entertain her neighbors by singing and dancing for them. Reynolds loved performing and later went on to become one of Hollywood's most well-known actresses in the 1950s.

Although Debbie Reynolds said she loved growing up in El Paso and that she had a great childhood there, she didn't come back to visit often. She said that her visits made her sad since they were usually for funerals.

Reynolds did return to El Paso in 2010 to make an appearance at a screening of *Singin' in the Rain*. The film was aired at the Plaza Classic Film Festival. She spoke at the festival about her career and about growing up in El Paso. El Paso residents later praised her for her bravery in visiting again.

Debbie Reynolds died in 2016 in Los Angeles. She suffered from a stroke just one day after her daughter, *Star Wars* actress Carrie Fisher, passed away.

A Popular Country Band Was Named After the State

You probably figured out by now that the country band Lonestar was named after the Lone Star State. But do you know why?

Well, let's go back to the band's beginning. It may surprise you to know that Lonestar wasn't the band's first name. The band originally started out as Texassee. This name came about because all of the members of the group were from Texas. They also all somehow met each other while they were in Texas. However, it wasn't until band members Richie and Dean ran into one another in Nashville that they got the idea to start a band. After they had the idea, they called band members Michael and Keech to come out to Nashville.

In case you haven't already figured it out, Texassee was the result of Texas + Tennessee. Get it? Yeah, the record label thought the name was pretty lame, too.

When the band got a record deal, one of the conditions of the deal was that they would need to change their name. One of their songwriters told the producer of the album that they should choose a band name that would let people know they were all from Texas. That's how the name Lonestar was born.

The band has had several No. 1 singles, but they're most well-known for their songs "Amazed" and "I'm Already There."

Willie Nelson Has an Unusual Favorite Texas Childhood Pastime

We've heard of celebrities with some really unusual favorite pastimes. For example, Mike Tyson is said to have loved racing pigeons when he was younger, while Johnny Depp has a collection of Barbie dolls he plays with. But Texas country singer Willie Nelson's favorite pastime just might take the cake in terms of weirdness.

Nelson, who grew up in Abbott, loved to fight bumble bees when he was a kid. *Uh… what?*

Willie Nelson said he and his friends would go to fields where they would fight off swarms of bumblebees. They would get stung so much that their eyes would swell shut.

We can't imagine how this would be any fun, but apparently, his days of bumblebee fighting brings him fond memories.

Willie Nelson blames it on his small-town upbringing. He told *The New York Times*, "That shows how bored you can get in Abbott."

Apparently, he loved bumblebees so much that he mentions them in a line of his song, "Crazy Like Me."

We wonder if his favorite Texas adult pastime is walking down the street that's named after him. The city of Austin paid homage to the singer by naming a street downtown after him!

RANDOM FACTS

1. Though he was raised in Tennessee, R&B singer Usher was born in Dallas, Texas. He later went on to play in the 2001 movie titled *Texas Rangers*!

2. *Desperate Housewives* actress Eva Longoria's hometown is Corpus Christi. When she was in high school, she worked at a local Wendy's. In 2008, she returned to Wendy's to work the counter for a day.

3. Actor Matthew McConaughey was born in Uvalde, Texas, and grew up in Longview, Texas. He went to Longview High School, where he was voted "Most Handsome" during his senior year. Later, after his rise to fame, McConaughey was reported for a domestic disturbance in Austin. Responders found him naked and playing the bongo. The actor was believed to be high on herbal intoxicants.

4. Willie Nelson, Carol Burnett, and Carolyn Jones (of *The Addams Family*) were all born in Texas during the same month!

5. *Charlie's Angels* actress and former sex icon, Farrah Fawcett, was born in Corpus Christi. The actress attended the University of Texas and was

voted one of the 10 most beautiful coeds. After Fawcett died of colon cancer in 2009, the friends she grew up with in Corpus Christi remembered her as "bubbly, smart, funny, athletic, and a loyal friend," according to the *Daily Herald*.

6. Texas-born Jessica Simpson may be from the country, but she hasn't always been down with her roots. Simpson once forgot the lyrics to a Dolly Parton song that she performed at a tribute event for the musician. However, Dolly forgave her and later sang on a track of Simpson's country album, *Do You Know.*

7. Selena Gomez was named after the late Selena Quintanilla-Perez. It's amazing how much the two have in common: both Texans, both with Mexican heritage, and both talented musicians.

8. Jared Padalecki and Jensen Ackles both spoke in favor of David's Law, which has since passed. The Texas law, which was named after a teen who committed suicide, criminalizes cyberbullying and requires schools to follow protocol.

9. Although *The Texas Chain Saw Massacre* is based on actual events, you may be surprised to learn that its inspiration doesn't come from Texas at all. The movie is actually based on Wisconsin serial killer Ed Gein.

10. *Gilmore Girls* and *Sisterhood of the Traveling Pants* actress Alexis Bledel is Tejano. She was born and raised in Houston, but her mom is from Mexico. The actress told *Latina Magazine* that while people usually mistake her as Irish, her family has embraced the Mexican culture. The actress told *Latina Magazine* that they speak Spanish in her parents' home and her mom "cooks amazing Mexican food."

11. Sandra Bullock, who lives in Texas, owns Walton's Fancy and Staple in Austin. It's an upscale restaurant, bakery, floral shop, and event planning business.

12. There was a TV show based on Dallas, Texas, and you've probably heard of it. *Dallas*, which aired from 1978 to 1991, was filmed in Frisco, Texas, which isn't too far away from Dallas. The show was filmed at the Cloyce Box Ranch.

13. *Teen Mom* star Farrah Abraham owns a frozen yogurt shop called FROCO FRESH & FROZEN in the Austin area.

14. Houston-born actress Jennifer Garner helped provide relief during Hurricane Harvey through the organization Save the Children, for which she's a trustee.

15. *Party of Five* and *I Know What You Did Last Summer* actress Jennifer Love Hewitt was born in Waco,

Texas. She won "Texas Our Little Miss Talent Winner," which led talent scouts to encourage her to pursue a career in acting. She later went on to star in the show *The Client List*, in which she plays a Texas woman who is struggling to make ends meet and turns to prostitution at a massage parlor. *The Client List* is loosely based on an actual prostitution scandal that happened in Odessa, Texas, in 2004.

16. Texan actor Jamie Foxx is a huge fan of the Dallas Cowboys. In fact, he originally hoped to play for the team. We wonder how different his career would have turned out.

17. Fred Gibson, who wrote the book *Old Yeller*, was a journalist in the late 1930s. He wrote for the *Corpus Christi Caller-Times*.

18. Country singer and Arlington native Maren Morris was given the title Chairwoman for the Texas Music Project, a non-profit organization that helped her become famous herself. The organization helps provide music education to disadvantaged groups. Texas Music Project sent Morris to a Grammy songwriting class in California.

19. *Fast and the Furious* actress Michelle Rodriguez grew up in San Antonio. She has fond memories of her mom's Spanish band playing in Brackenridge Park.

20. Musician Austin Mahone was born and raised in San Antonio. One of his first performances was at the Houston Rodeo in 2013, where he had the audience do the Harlem Shake. He performed with fellow Texan Demi Lovato. Mahone told *The Houston Chronicle* that he always gets Whataburger whenever he's back in Texas.

Test Yourself – Questions and Answers

1. Which famous singer was born and raised in Houston?

    a. Rihanna
    b. Britney Spears
    c. Beyoncé

2. Which of the following *Disney* childhood actresses did *not* play in *Barney & Friends*?

    a. Hilary Duff
    b. Selena Gomez
    c. Demi Lovato

3. Which city celebrates *Winnie-the-Pooh* character Eeyore's birthday?

    a. Corpus Christi
    b. Austin
    c. Dallas

4. Which actor from *Supernatural* recently opened a brewery in the Austin area?

    a. Jensen Ackles
    b. Jared Padalecki

5. Which Texas musician recorded a song with Dolly Parton?

    a. Maren Morris
    b. Jessica Simpson
    c. Beyoncé

Answers

1. c.
2. a.
3. b.
4. a.
5. b.

CHAPTER THREE

TEXAS INVENTIONS, IDEAS, AND MORE!

Have you ever wondered what businesses, products or inventions got started in Texas? Do you know which popular soda came from Texas? Which stores got their start in Texas? There are a number of things that may be a part of your daily life that originated from the Lone Star State. Some of them may even surprise you.

Dr Pepper

Most people either love it or hate it, but did you know that Dr Pepper originated in Waco, Texas? In fact, it's the oldest soft drink brand and the Dr Pepper Snapple Group is the oldest soft drink manufacturer in the United States!

Dr Pepper was invented by a pharmacist named Charles Alderton in 1885. He worked at Morrison's Old Corner Drug Store. While his job was to mix medications, Alderton also enjoyed creating new soft drink recipes at the drug store's soda fountain.

The first to taste-test Alderton's original recipe for Dr Pepper was Wade Morrison, the owner of the drug store. The owner liked the flavor of the drink as much as Alderton did, so they began offering it to store customers. Early customers began to call the drink "Waco" at first. They would ask for "a Waco" or "a shot of Waco."

Wade Morrison has been credited with naming Dr Pepper. However, there's a lot of controversy over why he chose the name. According to the Dr Pepper Museum, which is located in Waco, there are 12 different theories.

The most popular theory is that it was named after an actual Dr. Pepper. It's been rumored that Pepper may have either given Morrison his first job or Morrison may have been in love with Pepper's daughter, though there's nothing on record that proves either theory.

Another possible theory is that it may have been given "Dr." to convince people that the soda was healthy. This was commonly used to trick people into buying products in the 1880s.

Despite the many theories that abound on how Dr Pepper got its name, no one knows for sure. It seems that it will forever remain a mystery!

Though the early spelling of the name was "Dr. Pepper", the period after "Dr" was later removed to make a stylistic statement. An early logo containing the period also made the logo difficult to read.

The recipe for Dr Pepper is a secret. However, a book of formulas and recipes that were believed to be from Morrison's Old Corner Drug Store was once discovered at an antique store in the Texas Panhandle. There was a recipe in the book called "D Peppers Pepsin Bitters", which people believed may have been an early recipe for Dr Pepper. Dr Pepper Snapple Group denied that this was a recipe for the soda. The company has also denied claims that Dr Pepper contains prune juice.

Slurpee's and Frozen Margaritas

The international convenience store chain 7-Eleven opened its first location in Dallas, Texas in 1927. In fact, this was the very first convenience store in America. When 7-Eleven first opened, it sold grocery store staples like eggs and milk, as well as blocks of ice. The following year, it also began to sell gasoline and other convenience items. In 1965, 7-Eleven began selling the Slurpee, which was first called the "ICEE."

The Slurpee later became the inspiration for the frozen margarita. The margarita itself had already been invented in Mexico, but the frozen margarita originated in Texas. The first frozen margarita machine, which can now be found at the Smithsonian, was invented in 1971. It was created by a restaurateur named Mariano Martinez who drew his inspiration from the Dallas 7-Eleven.

According to *The Dallas Morning News*, Martinez said, "I had a sleepless night and the next day, I stopped to get a cup of coffee at 7-Eleven and I saw that Slurpee machine. The entire concept hit me at one time."

The Underwire Bra

Bras come in so many shapes and sizes today. It's hard to think that, at one point, they didn't even have underwire bras. We can thank Texas for its invention.

Howard Hughes' son, Howard Hughes, Jr., was an inventor and filmmaker himself. The Houston native is credited with developing the first workable underwire bra.

Hughes' invention was first introduced to the world in the movie he made, *The Outlaw*. The bra was worn by Jane Russell. Russell wasn't impressed with the underwire bra. She claimed that it hurt so much that she ended up secretly taking it off and stuffing tissues in her regular bra.

Despite the actress's disappointment with the bra, the underwire bra still took off. It likely became popular due to two reasons: 1) The amount of publicity it received thanks to the movie, and 2) The discontinuance of metal rationing once World War II had ended.

Microchips

Today, we take our cell phones, computers, tablets, and other electronics for granted. You may not realize this, but you can actually thank a Dallas-based electronics company for your ability to use these items.

Texas Instruments, which is based in Dallas, designed the first microchip. It introduced its invention to the world in 1959 at the Radio Engineers' annual trade show in New York City.

The crazy part about it all was that no one realized what a huge invention this was at the time. No one had a clue that microchips would become the foundation of all the electronics we use today.

Whole Foods

Whole Foods is one of the most well-known high-end, natural-food supermarket chains in the country. With over 80,000 employees and more than 400 locations across the world, the store has been ranked as one of the top 100 places to work. And we get it. What other grocery store chain hires certified cheese professionals? (In order to qualify, one must receive their certification from the American Cheese Society, in case you're wondering).

You probably know that Whole Foods sells organic products to health-conscious customers. All of their meat is free of hormones and antibiotics. The store has a ban on foods containing high fructose corn syrup—along with 100 other ingredients!

But did you know that the first Whole Foods opened in Austin? It all started back in 1980 when four Austin grocers decided to band together to create the supermarket. Over time, the company began to add more locations in Texas, neighboring states, the rest of the United States, and now stores can even be found in other countries.

The Whole Foods store located in Austin remains the largest store in the entire chain. It encompasses 80,000 square feet of space, a rooftop ice skating rink, and a full bar that you can drink at, once you've finished grocery shopping. You can go grocery shopping, ice skating, and enjoy an alcoholic beverage all in one place on the same day.

Pace Picante Sauce

If you love salsa, you've probably heard of Pace Picante Sauce. The Pace Foods Company was started in 1947 by David Pace. Despite growing up in Louisiana, Pace ended up in San Antonio due to pilot-training school during World War II.

Pace began his business with syrups, jams, and jellies. However, he decided that the "real syrup of the

Southwest" was Mexican picante sauce. Today, most of us refer to this as just "salsa."

David Pace tried a unique form of marketing his picante sauce. He would take it to restaurants with him and then leave it behind for other people to try.

Pace was known for creating a "No Heat" jalapeno, which he used in his mild products. It gives the salsa its flavor without delivering an overabundance of spice.

Pace Foods is located in Paris, Texas. Today, some of the specialty sauces they are known for, besides their picante sauce, include their Salsa Verde, Mexican Four Cheese Salsa con Queso, Pico de Gallo, Pineapple Mango Chipotle Salsa, and Black Bean & Roasted Corn Salsa.

In 1995, the company was bought out by the Campbell Soup Company.

Weed Eater

The Weed Eater was invented in Houston by George Ballas, the grandfather of professional dancer, Mark Ballas, of *Dancing with the Stars* fame.

The idea came to Ballas one day when he was working in the yard and took a break to wash the car. The spinning nylon bristles of an automatic car wash gave him the idea to design a similar product, which would protect the bark of the trees that he was weed trimming around.

He sought investors, but no one thought the invention was worth anything. Still, Ballas persisted and put his own money into his idea. It all turned out to be worth it in the end. In 1977, he sold his company for a whopping $80 million.

Dell Computers

Dell is one of the most well-known computer brands in existence today. You've probably even owned one at some point in time. Did you know that the company got its start in Austin?

Dell Computers was started by Michael Dell. He built the first Dell in his off-campus dorm room at the University of Texas at Austin in 1984. Michael Dell ended up dropping out of college during his freshman year to focus on his business. He did this after receiving just $1,000 from his family!

It all paid off in the end. In 2014, Michael Dell's net worth was estimated to be a whopping $18 billion.

The very first Dell computer sold for $795. During Dell's first year, the company grossed over $73 million.

Breast Implants

Have you ever wondered who the brains behind breast implants were? Well, the mystery has been solved. You can thank two doctors from Houston for changing the world of plastic surgery forever.

Doctors Frank Gerow and Thomas Cronin were the geniuses behind breast implants. It was after squeezing a blood bag that Gerow came up with the idea of a silicone breast.

Wondering who the first guinea pig was? Well, the very first implant was done on a dog named Esmerelda. Though Esmerelda ended up chewing at her stitches a couple of weeks later, requiring the breast implant to be removed, the operation was considered successful.

Fast forward to spring of 1962 when Timmie Jean Lindsey, a mother of six, underwent surgery to have silicone breast implants inserted at Jefferson Davis Hospital in Dallas, Texas.

While the doctors were pleased with the results of the surgery, they had no idea that their invention would be what it is today. Thomas Biggs, a junior plastic surgery resident at the time, told *BBC*, "Sure it was a little bit exciting, but if I'd had a mirror to the future I'd have been dumbstruck."

It's thought that breast implants gained so much traction because the 1950s brought about cultural changes that included a societal expectation of bigger breasts.

As of 2012, it was estimated that somewhere between

1.5-2.5 million women had received breast implants in the past decade.

Liquid Paper

Liquid paper, which is used to eliminate mistakes from papers, comes in many brands today. One of the most popular versions of the product is Wite-Out. Well, you can thank a woman from Texas for the invention.

In the 1950s, a typist named Bette Nesmith Graham came up with the idea behind Liquid Paper because she needed to figure out a way to prevent one typo from ruining an entire page of typing. Her invention included tempera paint, which she mixed in her kitchen.

Graham first started selling the product as "Mistake Out" from her home in 1956.

Her invention was so successful that Gillette bought it in 1979, for $47 million.

Fritos

There's a reason Texans love their Frito pie! Fritos originated from Texas.

You might think Fritos and corn chips were invented at the same time, but this couldn't be further from the truth. Corn chips originated in Mexico.

It was during the Depression that Charles Elmer

Doolin, a confectioner from San Antonio, bought a bag of fried chips at a local gas station. Doolin decided to come up with his own recipe.

As it turns out, Doolin's recipe was a hit. Fritos made their way to restaurants throughout Dallas and even to Disneyland.

In 1959, Doolin teamed up with Herman Lay. Together, the two of them formed the Frito-Lay company. The company now produces Doritos, Cheetos, Tostitos, Ruffles, and other beloved snack foods. Frito-Lay's headquarters are in Plano, Texas.

You can get a Frito pie, which is a bag of Fritos with a scoop of chili and cheese, at the Texas State Fair!

Fajitas

Have you ever wondered who invented fajitas?

Since it's one of the most popular menu items at a Mexican restaurant, most people think that Mexico is to credit for the invention of fajitas. However, fajitas actually come from Texas—and the history of the recipe goes way back.

Fajitas were invented in the 1930s, in Texas's Rio Grande Valley. It's thought that ranch hands and cowboys were the ones who created this recipe since they were often paid in meat trimmings. A fajita involves grilling meat (usually steak), peppers, and onions and serving it on a flour or corn tortilla.

However, it wasn't until 1969 that fajitas began to gain popularity. It was during this time that a guy named Sonny Falcon opened a fajita stand in Kyle, Texas. Once they began to gain traction, Tex-Mex restaurants began to add fajitas to their menus, even before they gained popularity throughout the world!

Ruby Red Grapefruit

Did you know that ruby red grapefruit didn't naturally occur? Believe it or not, no one actually meant for this variation of grapefruit to happen at all.

In 1929, the first ruby red grapefruit was found on a small orchard in Rio Grande Valley, Texas. Prior to its discovery, pink and white grapefruits weren't very popular. Both were too sour. However, this new grapefruit variety was different from all of the others, with its red flesh and sweeter taste.

In fact, ruby red grapefruit was enjoyed so much by the locals that *millions* of dollars were spent trying to figure out how to breed redder, sweeter versions of this fruit. The Rio Red, the Star Ruby, and the March Ruby all came about as a result of this effort.

Five years later, the grapefruit industry in Texas was booming, all thanks to its new, sweeter fruit!

Shopping Centers

Shopping is an American tradition, but did you know that shopping centers actually originated from Texas?

The very first shopping center was born in Dallas. The Highland Park Village, which opened in 1931, consisted of luxury retailers that were all built by one owner. What was unique about the Highland Park Village was that it was the first planned shopping center in the United States.

According to the Highland Park Village's website, it was "the first planned shopping center in the United States with a unified architectural style and stores facing in toward an interior parking area."

Today, some of the retailers that can be found at Highland Park Village include Anthropologie, Ralph Lauren, Tory Burch, Dior, Fendi, Cartier, Jimmy Choo, Starbucks, and more.

Corn Dogs

Nowadays, corn dogs can be found at just about any state fair. You can even buy them in your frozen foods section at most supermarkets. But did you know that corn dogs were first introduced in Texas?

In fact, corn dogs are one of the most popular attractions in the Texas State Fair's history. The Fletcher's Corny Dog was first sold at the fair in 1942 by the Fletcher brothers, Neil and Carl. It's believed that the ease of eating the corn dogs off a stick was part of the reason why they gained so much popularity. Fletcher's Corny Dogs have been tasted by everyone from Julia Child to Oprah Winfrey!

Since 1942, their menu has expanded. They have added a turkey dog option and have experimented with jalapeno cheese corn dogs.

In the 1980s, Fletcher's made a (failed) attempt at expanding their corn dog business by opening franchise locations in Texas and a few other states. They have since decided that they will remain selling only at the Texas State Fair for now.

Bill Fletcher, one of the current owners of Fletcher's, says that the recipe is a family secret—and it's no wonder! Approximately 400,000 corn dogs are sold at the Texas State Fair each year.

RANDOM FACTS

1. Cookies 'n cream was first mass-produced by Blue Bell Creameries, which is headquartered in Brenham, Texas. The idea came about after one of the Blue Bell employees sampled the flavor at an ice cream parlor. Though Blue Bell doesn't claim to be the brains of the idea, they were the first to have the idea patented and were also the first to gain rights to use Oreos in their ice cream.

2. The balloon-expendable stent, which is used to unclog blocked vascular vessels during coronary surgery, was invented at the University of Texas Health Science Center. It was invented by Julio Palmaz, a doctor of vascular radiology. He received a patent in 1985, which was recognized as one of the "Ten Patents that Changed the World" of the century.

3. Despite what its name might lead you to believe, the popular franchise Texas Roadhouse did *not* start in Texas. It wasn't even started by a Texan. Texas Roadhouse is headquartered in Louisville, Kentucky—which is where its owner is also from. That being said, Texans are huge fans of Texas Roadhouse. There are more Texas Roadhouse store franchises in Texas than in any

other state. Willie Nelson even owns a Texas Roadhouse franchise in Austin!

4. Automatic Teller Machines, or ATMs, were designed by Don Wetzel of a Dallas-based firm called Docutel. Although Wetzel didn't invent the first ATM, he's responsible for their ability to provide you with information about your account balance, deposit money, and so on.

5. The first full drive-in movie theater was opened in Comanche, Texas in 1921. The drive-in theater played silent films.

6. Ammonia-free hair color was invented in Texas, but it wasn't invented by a Texan. It was created by Farouk Shami, who had moved from Palestine to Houston. He ventured into the hair product business when he moved to Texas, but he had a severe allergy to ammonia. His company, BioSilk, has accommodated celebrity customers such as Courtney Cox and Madonna and now earns $1 billion a year.

7. Mary Kay Cosmetics was started in Dallas in 1963 by a woman named Mary Kay Ash. She started the company with just $5,000! Today, Mary Kay Cosmetics is the sixth-largest direct-sales company in the entire world.

8. 3-D printing was invented in the 1980s by a University of Texas alumnus, who founded the

method selective laser sintering, or SLS. Today, 3-D printing is used to create everything from bionic ears to organs.

9. The TopsyTail, which was designed to create an inverted ponytail, was an invention that came straight out of Texas. Dallas inventor Tomima Edmark was the brains behind the TopsyTail, which was all the rage in the early '90s.

10. Chain restaurant Chili's was started in Dallas, Texas. Larry Levine opened the first Chili's Bar & Grill in Dallas in 1975.

11. Speaking of chili, did you know that chili itself originated from Texas? It was thought to be a staple of travelers in the 1850s. During those days, travelers would form bricks out of dried beef, suet, chili peppers, and salt, which they would later boil during their travels. It later evolved into the chili con carne that we know today. This fall season, comfort food was first sold in the late 1800s at the San Antonio Chili Stand. Since San Antonio was a tourist hotspot, the stand was instrumental in the future popularity of the dish in both the West and South. In 1977, chili was declared Texas's official state dish.

12. Whataburger is a burger chain that can be found in Southern states, ranging from Florida to

Arizona. The first Whataburger was opened in Corpus Christi in 1950 by Harmon Dobson. It has been said that Dobson's goal was to make a burger so good that you would say, "What a burger!" The first Whataburger to be opened with its iconic orange-and-white striped, A-frame building was in Odessa, TX. Today, there are over 800 locations.

13. In 1967, a group of engineers at Texas Instruments, Inc., were given eight years to design the first hand-held electronic calculator. A patent for the calculator was issued to the company in 1974.

14. Scoop Away Clean Clumping cat litter was invented by San Antonio inventor William Mallow. Mallow also helped out with perfecting the formula of Graham's Liquid Paper.

15. Though Gatorade was designed to help prevent dehydration in Florida Gators football team players, it was founded by Dr. Robert Cade, who was born and raised in San Antonio. Dr. Cade was a medicine and nephrology professor at the University of Florida. After he was approached by the assistant Gators coach, who inquired about the cause as to why his players weren't urinating when they played football, Cade developed the rehydration drink with help from a team of research doctors.

16. Elevator music got its start in Dallas. It all began in the Statler Hilton. The idea behind elevator music was that no one would have to talk to each other when they were in elevators.

17. Contrary to what you might think, German chocolate cake didn't actually come from Germany! The first known reference to German chocolate cake was in an issue of the *Dallas Morning Star* in 1957. The cake was named after Samuel German, who created the dark baking chocolate that was used in the original recipe.

18. Car radios were designed in the 1920s by Dallas inventor Henry Garrett. Now we know who we can blame for hearing the same songs over and over again.

19. Tito's Vodka was created by Bert Butler "Tito" Beveridge II, a Texas native. Sales of his vodka were slow when his company opened in 1997. However, sales gained major traction in 2001 after Tito's Vodka won the Double Gold Medal for vodka at the San Francisco World Spirits Competition. The vodka beat more than 70 high-priced brands.

20. The idea of serving nachos at sports stadiums started in 1976 at a Texas Rangers game. Frank Liberto came to the realization that diluting cheese sauce with water and jalapeno juice

would be a cheap way to turn a profit. Other stadiums soon caught on to the idea and it's now one of America's favorite game-time snacks.

Test Yourself – Questions and Answers

1. Which convenience store got its start in Texas?

    a. Wawa
    b. Sheetz
    c. 7-Eleven

2. Which snack food did *not* originate from Texas?

    a. Stadium nachos
    b. Corn chips
    c. Fritos

3. Who originally invented fajitas?

    a. The Indians of Texas
    b. Sam Houston
    c. Cowboys and ranch hands

4. Which restaurant chain did *not* start out in Texas?

    a. Texas Roadhouse
    b. Chili's
    c. Whataburger

5. Which soda got its start at a drug store in Waco, Texas?

    a. Dr Pepper
    b. Root beer
    c. Mr. Pibb

Answers

1. c.
2. b.
3. c.
4. a.
5. a.

CHAPTER FOUR

TEXAS SPORTS: FOOTBALL, RODEO, AND MORE!

You probably know that Texans are crazy about their sports. In fact, it's been said that no state loves football the way Texas does. With not just one but *two* NFL teams, most people in Texas live and breathe football. But did you know that football isn't the official sport of Texas? Do you know which sport is? Read on to find out the answers to these questions and other interesting facts about sports in Texas!

Texas is Home to Many Professional Sports Teams

Did you know that of all the states, Texas has the second-highest number of professional sports teams? The only state with more professional sports teams than Texas is California.

Texas has two National Football League (NFL) teams: the Dallas Cowboys and the Houston Texans.

The state is home to three National Basketball Association (NBA) teams: The San Antonio Spurs, the Houston Rockets, and the Dallas Mavericks.

The state's Major League Baseball (MLB) teams include the Texas Rangers and the Houston Astros.

There are two Major League Soccer (MLS) teams in Texas. They are the FC Dallas and the Houston Dynamo.

The Dallas Stars are the only National Hockey League (NHL) team in the entire state.

That's a lot of sports teams! And it's not even counting the state's professional women's sports teams and its unprofessional sports teams.

Texas is also known for its college football teams, the University of Texas Longhorns and the Texas A&M University's Aggies.

The Dallas Cowboys Are Worth a Lot of Money, But Jerry Jones is *Not* the Richest NFL Team Owner

It may come as no surprise to you to learn that the Dallas Cowboys are worth *a lot* of money.

In fact, according to a 2015 article from *Forbes*, the Dallas Cowboys have been the top-earning NFL team for the past 18 years. In 2015, *Forbes* stated that the team was valued at $4 billion. In 2014 alone, the team earned $620 million in revenue.

So, why are the Dallas Cowboys the most valuable team in the NFL? Well, in 2014, the team had the highest number of people attend their games. They earned $120 million in premium-seating revenue. The Dallas Cowboys' stadium also earns money from non-NFL events. Those figures, though, don't include the amount of money Dallas Cowboys fans spend on memorabilia!

It's just another sign of how much Texans as a whole love football in comparison to those who live in other states.

You might be surprised to learn that Jerry Jones, the owner of the Dallas Cowboys, is *not* the richest NFL team owner. According to *Forbes*, Jerry Jones's net worth is a whopping $5 billion, but the richest is Paul Allen, who owns the Seattle Seahawks and has an estimated net worth of $17.8 billion. Jones ranks as the 5th richest NFL team owner.

Friday Night Lights Is Based on a Real High School Football Team in Texas

You've probably heard of the football-oriented TV show *Friday Night Lights*, starring Kyle Chandler and Connie Britton. Did you know the Emmy award-winning show is actually based on a real Texas high school football game?

The show is based on a 1990 non-fiction book called

Friday Night Lights: A Town, a Team, and a Dream by H. G. Bissinger.

The TV show centers on the fictional town of Dillon, Texas, and its high school football team, the Dillon Panthers.

However, the book was written about Odessa, Texas's Permian High School Panthers football team of 1988. The reason Bissinger chose to write about the town of Odessa was that he set off in search of a town where high school football was the most important thing. He spent the football season in Odessa with the coaches, players, and their families to garner appropriate research for the book.

There was a lot of backlash from Odessa residents after H. G. Bissinger published *Friday Night Lights: A Town, a Team, and a Dream*. He was supposed to do a book signing after its publication, but he had to cancel it due to threats of bodily harm. The residents were upset that Bissinger talked about the racism and misplaced academic priorities in the football-obsessed town.

All that being said, H. G. Bissinger's portrayal was fairly accurate. For many Texans, there's nothing more important than high school football.

The Super Bowl Has Been Held in Houston

Due to the state's love of football, it should be no surprise that the Super Bowl has been hosted in

Houston on more than one occasion!

The first time the Super Bowl was ever hosted in Houston was in 1974 at Rice Stadium. That year, the Minnesota Vikings beat the Miami Dolphins. The score was 24-7. It was the second year in a row the Vikings had played in the Super Bowl.

In 2004, the Super Bowl was again hosted in Houston, this time at Reliant Stadium. The New England Patriots won against the Carolina Panthers by a score of 32-29.

The last time the Super Bowl was held in Houston was in 2017. That year, the Super Bowl was hosted at NRG Stadium. Houston seems to be a lucky city for the New England Patriots because they won the Super Bowl *again* that year. They defeated the Atlanta Falcons by 34-28.

The Super Bowl Came to Be Because of a Texan

Did you know the Super Bowl wouldn't be the Super Bowl if it weren't for a Texan?

Okay, so the Super Bowl itself wasn't actually created in Texas. However, the *name* of the Super Bowl was invented by a Texan.

The term "Super Bowl" was coined by Lamar Hunt, American Football League Founder, Kansas City Chiefs owner, and then Dallas resident.

Hunt mentioned the idea at an NFL owner's meeting.

That was in the 1960s. The name wasn't actually official – as in printed on game tickets – until 1970. The Super Bowl had already been played three times before it officially received a name.

Hunt said that he was actually joking about the name, crediting his kids' Wham-O Superballs for the idea.

It's Not Easy to Become a Dallas Cowboys Cheerleader

Dallas is known for its gorgeous cheerleaders. If your dream is to become a Dallas Cowboys Cheerleader, you should know that it's not easy. In fact, the process of becoming and staying a cheerleader for this dream squad is pretty grueling!

There are a number of qualifications one must meet in order to become a Dallas Cowboys Cheerleader. While there are no height and weight requirements, cheerleaders need to look well-proportioned and should be "lean" enough to look good in the uniform.

During auditions, potential cheerleaders are quizzed on their knowledge of sports, nutrition, and the history of the Dallas Cowboys.

Judges will also make their selections based on the following: dance technique, figure, personality, high kicks, poise, enthusiasm, showmanship, and more.

Once a Dallas Cowboys Cheerleader has been

selected, she will need to continue to work hard to maintain her position. Dallas Cowboys Cheerleaders practice 20 to 30 hours per week, with most cheerleaders having other jobs. Not only will cheerleaders need to remain fit, but they must also choose a look they plan to stick with for the entire season. All tattoos are required to be covered.

Demi Lovato once reportedly said during an interview that her mom, a former Dallas Cowboys Cheerleader, said the squad wasn't even allowed to get a drink of water—even when they were dying of thirst!

In addition to being able to meet physical and performance requirements, Dallas Cowboys Cheerleaders are also trained in etiquette and interview techniques. A lot of the girls from the team use their positions to help raise money for charities.

Famous Dallas Cowboys Cheerleaders

There are a number of Dallas Cowboys Cheerleaders who have gone on to become famous through other endeavors.

Perhaps one of the most well-known former Dallas Cowboys Cheerleaders is Melissa Rycroft. After she left the team, she appeared as a contestant on *The Bachelor*. After that, she competed on the 8th season of the show *Dancing with the Stars*, which she won.

Another one of the most well-known former Dallas Cowboys Cheerleaders is Erica Kiehl Jenkins, a member of the Pussycat Dolls.

Bonnie-Jill Laflin is another former Dallas Cowboys Cheerleader who rose to fame after she was a part of the team in the 90s. She went on to have a recurring role in both *Baywatch* and *Ally McBeal*. She also starred in Dierks Bentley's music video for "Come a Little Closer."

Jill Marie Jones is a former Dallas Cowboys Cheerleader who later went on to star in the hit show *Girlfriends*.

Texas Hosts Two Bowl Games

The Sun Bowl, which generally takes place at the end of December, is held in El Paso every year. It's a college football bowl game. It's one of the oldest bowl games in the country. The only bowl game that's older than the Sun Bowl is California's Rose Bowl.

The first Sun Bowl was held on New Year's Day in 1935. At that point, it was held between high school football teams. It wasn't until the following year that the bowl was held for college football teams.

Hyundai is the current sponsor of the Sun Bowl. It bought naming rights to the game, which it will sponsor until 2019. Until that point, the game is called the Hyundai Sun Bowl.

Texas also hosts the Cotton Bowl Classic, another college bowl game that has taken place annually since 1937. It's currently known as the Goodyear Cotton Bowl Classic due to sponsorship reasons. It's held at the Cowboys Stadium in Arlington.

Surprisingly, Football is *Not* Texas's State Sport

If you're a Dallas Cowboys fan, you might be surprised to learn that Texas's state sport is *not* football. This seems nearly impossible, considering how much Texans love their football.

So, what *is* the state sport? Rodeo, which became the official state sport in 1997!

You may be wondering how rodeo got to be so popular in the Lone Star State. Well, rodeo dates back as far as the 1500s, when the Spanish and Mexican settlers introduced horses and cattle to the Southwest.

The word "rodeo" originated from the word vaquero. It means "round-up". Many of the rodeo skills that cowboys compete with today are skills that assisted cowboys and ranch hands during their round-ups.

It wasn't until after the Civil War that rodeo really started to grow in popularity. With the influx of wild cattle in the Southwest and a market for them in the East, cattle drives were born. Cattle ranches began to grow in popularity and so did cowboys.

During this time period, cowboys would hold informal competitions during the cattle and steer round-ups. At that point in time, there were no prizes involved in these competitions. Cowboys participated in rodeo style events as a form of entertainment.

Those early rodeo competitions actually ended up hurting the sport as a whole. Since the cowboys were willing to do it for free, they weren't viewed seriously later on. They needed to break free of the image of doing it for entertainment in order for it to be taken seriously as a professional sport – especially a *paid* professional sport.

The first rodeo on record took place in Pecos, Texas, on the 4th of July in 1883. It was the first rodeo competition that involved cash prizes. Although rodeo events continued in Pecos, it wasn't until 1929 that the event began to run every year.

The first indoor rodeo event was held in Fort Worth in 1917!

The Rodeo Cowboys Association was founded in Houston in 1945.

A cowboy from Texas has been credited with developing steer wrestling. Bill Pickett came up with a method of bulldogging steers, which involved biting their upper lips and grabbing the steer's horns to throw it to the ground. He showed off his method at Texas fairs and rodeos before being contacted by an agent in 1904, who helped him tour the West.

Today, there are a number of standardized rodeo events. Aside from steer wrestling, there's also bareback riding, bull riding, calf roping, saddle bronc riding, and team roping. Bull riding is the most popular rodeo event.

The Texas Rodeo Cowboy Hall of Fame is located in the Fort Worth, Texas, historic district, Fort Worth Stockyards.

The Houston Rodeo is HUGE

The Houston Rodeo is a good example of the saying, "Everything is bigger in Texas." The Houston Livestock and Rodeo is the largest rodeo *in the entire world!*

Also known as RodeoHouston, the rodeo has been held at the NGR Stadium in Houston for 15 years. In 2017, a record-breaking 2.6 million people attended the rodeo, which is 20 days long.

The rodeo isn't the only thing you'll see. Prior to the rodeo show, there's a cattle roundup that takes place in Downtown Houston with a parade. You can also participate in the ConocoPhillips Rodeo Run, which consists of 5k and 10k walks and runs. Last, but certainly not least, there's the World's Championship Bar-B-Que Contest.

Aside from the rodeo competitions, you can expect to see a number of other events at RodeoHouston. Some of these events include livestock competitions and auctions, pig racing, shopping, and an international wine competition. There's also a carnival and shopping.

Although the rodeo gets a lot of criticism due to the potentially unfair treatment of animals, the Houston Rodeo takes good care of the animals. In fact, animals are examined by judges during the hours leading up to the competitions to make sure that they're healthy enough for each event. Afterwards, the animals are reexamined. If animals have been injured, they're treated.

Animals aren't the only thing you'll see at the Houston Rodeo. There are concerts held at the rodeo each year. Some of the many popular musicians who have performed at RodeoHouston in the past include Elvis Presley, Garth Brooks, Justin Bieber, Janet Jackson, Beyoncé, Selena, Ariana Grande, Bon Jovi, Kenny Chesney, Luke Bryan, and Bob Dylan.

The Richest Rodeo Cowboy of All Time is a Texas Native

Rodeo champion Trevor Brazile has been called the Michael Jordan of Rodeo and is known to be a "phenomenon with a rope." Brazile has won 23 titles worldwide.

Brazile is the richest cowboy in the history of the Professional Rodeo Cowboys Associations. As of 2015, he was the first rodeo cowboy to have ever earned $6 million.

Trevor Brazile was born and raised in Amarillo. His father, who was also a four-time rodeo finalist himself, was the one who encouraged Trevor to learn to rope from a young age. The skills his father taught Trevor helped him to excel in steer roping, tie-down roping, and team roping.

Brazile was later trained by Hall of Fame team roper Roy Cooper. It was through Cooper's training that Brazile developed the confidence and determination it took to turn him into the rodeo success he is today!

The "Rankest Bull of All Time" Died in Texas

The most famous bull of all time died in Texas. Bodacious, who weighed 1,800 pounds, has been called the "rankest bull of all time."

Bodacious was a part of the rodeo in 1993. He knocked out famous bull rider Cody Lambert. Many of the riders were determined to ride Bodacious because the bull could give them very high points. However, in order to earn the points, riders had to stay on the bull for eight seconds and that was a problem. Most riders couldn't stay on Bodacious for even a second!

After so many riders were injured by the bull, Bodacious retired after just two years in the rodeo.

In 1999, Bodacious was one of the few animals to have been inducted into the Professional Rodeo Cowboys Association Hall of Fame.

Bodacious died of kidney failure at Andrews Rodeo Company Ranch in Addielou, Texas, in May of 2000.

The Heisman Trophy Was Named After a Texas Coach...

The Heisman Trophy is an award that's given out each year to the most outstanding college football player in the United States whose performance demonstrates the "pursuit of excellence with integrity". It's presented prior to the postseason bowl games by the Heisman Trophy Trust.

The trophy was named after John Heisman, who was a coach and athletic director at Rice University in Houston. The award was renamed to honor Heisman following his death in 1936. Though it was originally only given to players "east of the Mississippi," it was expanded during this time to include players "west of the Mississippi" as well.

...and Players from Texas Have Won the Heisman Trophy!

Several Texas college football players have won the Heisman Trophy.

The Heisman Trophy was first given to a Texas player in 1957. The player was a Texas A&M Aggies halfback named John David Crow.

In 1977, the trophy was awarded to Texas Longhorns running back Earl Campbell.

A Texas Longhorns player named Ricky Williams was given the award in 1998.

In 2012, Texas A&M Aggies quarterback, Johnny Manziel, received the Heisman Trophy.

Of the four Texas college football players who won the Heisman Trophy, both John David Crow and Earl Campbell went on to be inducted into the College Football Hall of Fame.

George Foreman is From Texas

George Foreman is arguably the most well-known athlete from Texas. The former professional boxer is a two-time heavyweight champion, as well as an Olympic gold medalist. He competed between the years of 1969 and 1977 and then again between 1987 and 1997.

Foreman was born in Marshall, Texas. He grew up in Houston's Fifth Ward. George Foreman wrote in his autobiography, *By George: The Autobiography of George Foreman*, which he had a troubled childhood, even dropping out of high school. He took up amateur boxing, which led him to his future success.

While George Foreman had many achievements through boxing, it's not the only reason he's had so much success. Foreman is more well-known today for being the face of the George Foreman Grill. It's been estimated that Foreman made more than $200 million for endorsing it.

RANDOM FACTS

1. Of Texas's professional male sports teams, Dallas is home to five of them: the Dallas Cowboys, the Dallas Mavericks, FC Dallas, the Texas Rangers, and the Dallas Stars. It's also home to the women's NBA team, the Dallas Wings.

2. The Dallas Cowboys have played in the Super Bowl eight times, and they only lost three of those games. The Cowboys won during the years of 1971, 1977, 1992, 1993, and 1997.

3. The Dallas Cowboys are the only NFL team that had 20 consecutive winning seasons, which occurred between the years of 1966 and 1985.

4. The world's first covered, domed stadium can be found in Texas. The Astrodome, which is located in Houston, has been called the "Eighth Wonder of the World". The stadium, which opened in 1965, has hosted numerous sporting events, rodeos, and concerts. It was even used as a shelter for people who were evacuated due to Hurricane Katrina in 2005.

5. There are more than 1,300 football stadiums in Texas. This means there's enough room to seat over 4 million people! This is enough to seat all of

the people living in the state of Oklahoma or the country of Panama.

6. The oldest high school football stadium is Lang Field, which belongs to St. Anthony's Catholic High School. It's the home stadium of the St. Anthony's Yellow Jackets.

7. Football player Earl Campbell has played for the Texas Longhorns, the Houston Oilers, and the John Tyler Lions. Combined, he ran 15,582 yards—or 8.8 miles—for the Texas football teams he's played for.

8. Former Dallas Cowboys quarterback Tony Romo has participated in many Dallas-area charity events, with organizations like the Make-A-Wish Foundation, the United Way, and the Society for the Prevention of Cruelty to Animals.

9. Tony Romo was mentioned in *Forbes*'s 2007 list of America's Most Eligible Bachelors. He was also voted as the Sexiest Male Athlete in a list put out by Victoria's Secret in 2008.

10. Dallas Cowboys Hall of Famers Emmitt Smith and Michael Irvin had the most successful running back/wide receiver season of all time. In 1995, the two were the first and only running back and wide receiver who, together, ran 1,600+ yards in just one season.

11. Roy Rogers once visited the Houston Rodeo in 1956. He wore a fake mustache, glasses, and a fireman's uniform while he checked out the livestock exhibits because he was afraid of being mobbed by fans.

12. World champion road racing cyclist Lance Armstrong is from Plano, Texas. Though he's known today for cycling, he actually began his athletic career as a swimmer for the City of Plano Swim Club—and a talented one, at that! He finished 4th place in the state competition in the 1,500-meter freestyle.

13. The Texas Sports Hall of Fame Museum is located in Waco, Texas. Some of the things you can see at the museum include the Texas Hall of Fame Gallery, a Cotton Bowl Exhibit, the Southwest Conference Gallery, the Dave Campbell Library, and the Tom Landry Theater.

14. In 1947, Gene Autry was a part of the downtown Houston Rodeo parade.

15. Some of the earliest baseball cards in existence portray players from the Texas League. These baseball card sets, which were released in 1910, are called "Old Mill" and "Mello-Mint, The Texas Gum."

16. Carl Lewis, who won nine gold Olympic medals over the course of four Olympics, lived in

Houston. The athlete was inducted into the Track and Field Coaches Association Hall of Fame in 2016.

17. Texas Motor Speedway is home to one of the biggest TV screens in the entire world. The screen, which is called "Big Hoss," is more than 20,600 square feet. When it was unveiled in 2014, it was the largest HD LED screen in the world. However, it has since been surpassed by a TV screen at the NFL Jacksonville Jaguar's EverBank Field.

18. Jack Johnson, who was the first black man to hold a Heavyweight Championship, came from Galveston. He held the title from 1908 to 1915.

19. Mia Hamm is a retired pro soccer player who won two Olympic gold medals and twice helped the United States win the FIFA Women's World Cup. Hamm grew up in Wichita Falls and has been inducted into the Texas Sports Hall of Fame.

20. Retired NBA legend Shaquille O'Neal went to high school in San Antonio! He helped his high school basketball team win the state championship. He still holds the Texas high school basketball team record of 791 rebounds.

Test Yourself – Questions and Answers

1. Which famous athlete was *not* born and raised in Texas?

   a. George Foreman
   b. Michael Jordan
   c. Shaquille O'Neal

2. What is Texas's official state sport?

   a. Football
   b. Baseball
   c. Rodeo

3. The Houston Livestock and Rodeo is the largest rodeo in:

   a. The entire world
   b. The United States
   c. The state of Texas

4. What was the name of the famous bull who died in Texas?

   a. Bootylicious
   b. Bodacious
   c. Bronx

5. The book *Friday Night Lights: A Town, a Team, and a Dream* by H. G. Bissinger was written about which high school football-obsessed town in Texas?

   a. Abilene
   b. El Paso
   c. Odessa

Answers

1. b.
2. c.
3. a.
4. b.
5. c.

CHAPTER FIVE

TEXAS'S UNSOLVED MYSTERIES, SUPERNATURAL, AND OTHER WEIRD FACTS

Just about every state has at least one unsolved mystery. Have you ever wondered what unsolved mysteries, murders or weird crimes have happened in Texas? Have you heard about the scandal that affected one town's high school in Texas? Do you know what creepy folklore haunts the state? What crimes in Texas have affected the entire United States? Read on to find out what scary, eerie or just otherwise weird or bizarre things have happened in Texas.

Jack the Ripper May Be Tied to Texas

You've probably heard of the London serial killer Jack the Ripper by now. But did you know that Jack the Ripper may somehow be linked to another serial killer who murdered people in Texas?

In the late 1800s, there was a serial killer in Austin who came to be known as "The Servant Girl Annihilator." The killer was responsible for eight axe murders in the city between the years of 1884 and 1885. The first few people who were murdered were servants, but later victims were not. Though the killings were referred to as the Servant Girl Murders, one of the girls' male partners was also a victim.

The murders only stopped after private investigators were brought in to solve the case. It was believed that the killer only stopped the murders out of fear of getting caught. Although there were a number of people questioned, none of them were actually tried for murders.

Three years later, the Jack the Ripper murders began to happen in the Whitechapel district of London.

It's a popular belief that the Servant Girl Annihilator and Jack the Ripper may have been the same person. There are two different theories about how this killer struck in both Austin and London. Was the killer from Texas, London, or somewhere else entirely?

The first theory involves a Malaysian cook named Maurice. The restaurant Maurice had worked at had been in the same neighborhood where most of the victims of the Servant Girl Murders had lived. Maurice told people he was going to London and he left in January 1886, just weeks after the murders had stopped in Austin. Some have theorized that he left Austin to prevent being caught for the Servant Girl Murders and set out to continue kills in a new place, leading him to go on to become Jack the Ripper. Was Maurice's departure merely a coincidence or did he end up in London?

There's another popular theory, which says that Jack the Ripper may have been visiting Austin at the time of the Servant Girl Murders. In her book *Jack the Ripper: The American Connection*, author Shirley Harrison tosses around this theory. She suggests that Liverpool-born James Maybrick, who is believed by many to be responsible for the Jack the Ripper killings based on his own controversial diary entries, was actually the Servant Girl Annihilator!

Harrison suggests that Maybrick was in Austin at the time of the Servant Girl Murders. He was later poisoned by his wife, who interestingly enough, was from the United States. Florence Maybrick was from Mobile, Alabama.

After she murdered her husband, there was never another homicide committed by either the Servant Girl Annihilator *or* Jack the Ripper ever again.

So, did Jack the Ripper really have a connection to Texas or was it merely just a coincidence? More than 100 years have passed and the world may never know.

Werewolf Sightings Have Been Reported in Texas

Are you a believer in the supernatural? If so, it might not surprise you to know that werewolf sightings have been reported in Texas. While werewolf sightings have been reported all over the country, there have been many more in Texas than other states.

Perhaps one of the most well-known werewolf reports comes out of Greggton, Texas, which is located near Longview. In a 1960 issue of *Fate Magazine*, a woman named Delburt Gregg detailed her encounter with a werewolf, which had taken place two years earlier.

Mrs. Gregg said she was home alone when she heard a scratching sound on the screen window in her bedroom during a thunderstorm. When lightning flashed, she saw what she called a "huge, shaggy, wolf-like creature" that glared at her with "baleful, glowing, slitted eyes."

Delburt Gregg said that as she ran to grab a flashlight, the wolf went to hide in her bushes. She waited for the animal to leave in hopes of seeing it again, but it never emerged from the bushes. Instead, she saw a man climb out of the bushes and walk down the street.

Another story comes out of Converse, Texas, though this one is a bit more controversial. It has been said that in the 1960s, a man sent his son hunting in the woods. The boy was stalked by the wolf and ran home. His father told him to go back. When the boy never came home later that night, a search party found a huge werewolf devouring his body. Though many are skeptical of the story, the "Wolf-Man of Converse" is still a legend in the town today.

In Kimble County, there's also a legend about an old Native American man who would take the form of a wolf to avoid being captured by cavalrymen. It was said that when he was cornered, he would turn into a wolf and attack, often injuring or even killing those who wanted to capture him.

Folklore or not, there are plenty of stories to tell by the campfire during your next trip to Texas!

The Amber Behind AMBER Alerts Was Murdered in Texas

Sure, you know about AMBER Alerts. Nowadays, you even get them sent to your smartphone. But do you know the story of how they began? Do you know about the girl who AMBER Alerts were named after?

Though AMBER stands for America's Missing: Broadcast Emergency Response, the Alert system was actually named after a real-life girl named Amber. She went missing in Texas in the '90s.

Amber Hagerman was a 9-year-old girl who was

kidnapped and murdered in Arlington in 1996. She was kidnapped when she was riding her bike with her brother in a grocery store parking lot. A blue truck was spotted leaving the scene.

Four days after Amber Hagerman went missing, a dog walker discovered her body floating in a creek a few miles away from the grocery store. Amber's throat had been slit.

Sadly, it's been more than 20 years and Amber Hagerman's death still remains a mystery. Who killed Amber? Sadly, no one knows. There have been no suspects in her murder. All police have to go on is a description that was given by a man who witnessed the abduction from his yard. The case still remains open to this day and every lead is treated as though it was the first.

Despite the fact that there haven't been answers in Amber Hagerman's death, some positivity has come out of the tragedy. As of November 2017, the AMBER Alerts system has helped bring home 897 children.

Amber Hagerman's story has been turned into a *Lifetime* movie called *Amber's Story*.

The Texas Cheerleading Scandal Made National Headlines

You may have heard of the *Lifetime* movie called *Fab Five: The Texas Cheerleader Scandal* starring Jenna

Dewan-Tatum and Ashley Benson, but did you know that it's actually based on a true story?

The real-life story took place in McKinney, Texas, when a group of spoiled cheerleaders known as the "fab five" made national headlines in 2005. Some have called them the Real Life *Mean Girls*. Others have referred to them as "girls gone wild." No matter how you look at it, these girls were downright rotten. They insulted teachers, skipped classes, and terrorized their coaches.

They gained attention when they posted racy photos wearing their cheerleading uniforms on Myspace. In the photos, the girls were wearing bikinis, showing off their underwear, and posing in a Condoms to Go shop while wearing their uniforms.

A teacher from their school even said the girls were more difficult to deal with than gang members.

Michaela Ward, the 4th cheerleading coach who the girls drove out in just one year, was the first coach to try to discipline the girls. Stories of what actually happened tended to be contradictive. The girls claimed that Ward tried to befriend them and stated that she didn't discipline them.

Regardless of what really happened, the girls publicly attacked the coach and claimed that she had made false allegations against them.

Michaela Ward told *Good Morning America* that the girls went as far as to send dirty text messages to Ward's husband and another coach.

Ward later sued the school for wrongful termination and defamation. She is still a cheerleading coach today.

So, how did these girls manage to get away with so much? The head ringleader's mother was the school principal, who undermined the coach for trying to discipline the cheerleaders. Ward said it wasn't only the principal to blame but the entire administration *and* parents who prevented the girls from being reprimanded.

One of the Most Famous Hate Crimes Took Place in Texas

One of the most famous, controversial, and horrendous hate crimes in all of American history took place in Jasper, Texas, on June 7th, 1998. It was on that day that James Byrd, Jr., an African-American man, was murdered by three white supremacists named Shawn Berry, Lawrence Russell Brewer, and John King.

The three men beat Byrd. They defecated and urinated on him before they chained his ankles to the back of a pickup truck and dragged him for about 1.5 miles. It was hitting a culvert that killed him by severing his head and arm. The autopsy report showed that Byrd lived through most of the trip and was conscious.

All three of Byrd's killers have been charged and convicted. Lawrence Russel Brewer was executed for the crime in 2011. Shawn Berry is currently on death row, awaiting appeals. Berry received a sentence of life in prison.

James Byrd, Jr.'s son, Ross Byrd, wasn't happy with all of these sentences. Ross Byrd has participated with *Murder Victims' Families for Reconciliation*, an organization that speaks out against the death penalty. Ross Byrd has actively campaigned to spare the lives of those who murdered his father. He told *Reuters*, "You can't fight murder with murder." Ross Byrd felt the killers should have spent their lives in prison.

James Byrd, Jr.'s death was one of the two hate crimes that led to the federal Matthew Shephard and James Byrd, Jr. Hate Crimes Act. The act, which is generally just referred to as the Matthew Shephard Act, was signed into law in 2009 by President Barack Obama.

A Serial Killer Struck in Texarkana in the 1940s

Have you heard of the movie *The Town That Dreaded Sundown*? The movie is loosely based on the Texarkana

Moonlight Murders that happened between February and May of 1946.

The serial killer, who came to be known as "The Phantom Killer" or "The Phantom Slayer," attacked eight people in a matter of 10 weeks. Five of those victims died. Contrary to popular belief, the Phantom Killer didn't only strike during a full moon. The killer did only attack during nighttime hours, however, which was what led the deaths to be called the "Moonlight Murders."

The murders caused a huge wave of panic throughout the town of Texarkana. People went out and stocked up on guns, ammunition, locks, and other forms of protection. People locked themselves in their homes at night, while many people's fear led them to leave town completely. While the Texas Rangers investigated the case, local teens tried to lure the killer.

There was one prime suspect in the case. Youell Swinney's wife described in great detail that he was responsible for two of the homicides. Since Mrs. Swinney refused to testify against him and later recanted her story, Swinney was never convicted of the crimes. However, two of the lead investigators in the case believed that Swinney was guilty.

One of the things that threw investigators off was that Swinney's fingerprints didn't match any of those connected with the homicides. It made some of the investigators wonder if Swinney's wife's story was credible.

Even so, Youell Swinney was arrested and imprisoned for selling cars. Though Swinney made multiple comments about knowing that he was wanted for more than just auto theft, he never made a formal confession to the crimes.

What makes the case even more mysterious was anonymous phone calls that were received by family members of the victims in 1999 and 2000. The caller claimed to be the daughter of the Phantom Killer and apologized for what her father had done. Swinney was not a father to any daughters.

Were those phone calls from the real Phantom Killer's daughter or were they only prank calls? To date, the case remains an unsolved mystery!

Four Teens Girls Were Murdered in a Texas Yogurt Shop

Four girls between the ages of 13 and 17 were murdered in a yogurt shop in Austin in 1991.

On December 6th, 1991, there was a fire at I Can't Believe It's Yogurt! Once the fire had been put out, the firefighters discovered the bodies of four teen girls, three of which were stacked in a pile.

Their names were Amy Ayers, Jennifer Harbison,

and sisters Sarah and Eliza Thomas. Eliza and Jennifer had been working the night shift when the other two girls stopped over to help close the yogurt shop.

When the girls were found, they were undressed and had been gagged and bound with their own clothes. They had all been shot in the head. The fire had burned their bodies. Detective Mike Huckabay compared the scene to things he had seen as a soldier in Vietnam.

Money had been stolen from the cash register, leading investigators to believe that the murders had started out as a robbery attempt that went awry.

The case proved to be difficult to solve. Since the killer had set the yogurt shop on fire, there was DNA from firefighters in the yogurt shop. Additionally, a lot of the evidence got washed away with water. Investigators have said that modern technological advances make it so the crime might have been easier to solve today, but things weren't so easy in 1991.

More than 50 people confessed to the yogurt shop murders. Police believe many of them to be mentally ill or seeking notoriety for the killings.

Kenneth Allen McDuff, a serial killer who was in the Austin area at the time of the homicides, was interviewed. However, authorities ruled him out as a suspect.

At one point, four suspects were charged with the murders. The suspects were Maurice Pierce, Robert Springsteen, Michael Scott, and Forest Welborn. Though they had been arrested eight days after the Yogurt Shop Murders, they weren't charged until eight years later.

Michael Scott and Robert Springsteen confessed to the murders, stating that it was a robbery that went wrong. Springsteen also confessed to raping one of the victims.

Charges were dropped against Welborn and Pierce. While investigators believed Pierce was the mastermind of the robbery/killings, there was no evidence that proved his involvement.

Both Scott and Springsteen went to trial. However, the charges against both Scott and Springsteen were dismissed in 2009. It was believed that they were coerced into making false confessions. There was no evidence against either suspect, and it was determined the trials were unfair.

The Austin Police Department had been planning for a retrial against the two when something surprising happened. New DNA evidence from an unknown man was found on one of the girl's bodies, throwing the entire case off.

As of 2016, the Austin Police Department is still continuing the investigation.

Austin Police Department Detective Jay Swann told *New York Post* that he still believes Springsteen and Scott were involved in the murders.

Swann also continues to believe that Maurice Pierce played a role in the murders. Maurice Pierce was killed in 2010, however. He stabbed a police officer during a traffic stop. The officer shot him.

The 1991 Yogurt Shop Murders have been the subject of three non-fiction novels: *Who Killed These Girls? Cold Case: The Yogurt Shop Murders* by Beverly Lowry, *See How Small* by Scott Blackwood, and *Murdered Innocents* by Corey Mitchell.

A Venomous Snake Once Went MIA in Austin

It was July of 2015 when a cobra went missing in Austin. Word of the snake being on the loose first got out when an 18-year-old man named Grant Thompson was discovered dead in his car.

Thompson worked at the Fish Bowl Pet Express, which his mother owned. When he was found, he had cobra bite marks on his arm, but the cobra was nowhere to be found.

Everyone in Austin was on the lookout for the snake, which ended up going viral during the hunt. Humorous tweets and memes of the cobra in tourist hotspots made their way around the Internet. Although jokes were cracked, the situation was really no laughing matter.

Grant Thompson's death was ruled a suicide, with autopsy reports showing that he didn't try to pull away from the snake. The venom led him to ultimately go into cardiac arrest. He also had a history of suicidal thoughts in the past.

After days spent searching for the snake, a driver found it located near the Lowe's Home Improvement store parking lot where Thompson's body was found.

We can imagine how much relief everyone in Austin felt once the snake was no longer on the loose!

An Alien May Have Died in Aurora, Texas

If you believe in the extraterrestrial, then the story of what happened on a farm near Aurora, Texas, may interest you.

In April of 1897, a UFO allegedly crashed into a windmill on a farm belonging to Judge J. S. Proctor. It was said that the pilot of the aircraft did not survive the accident and was buried at the Aurora Cemetery.

The incident was first reported in the *Dallas Morning News*. The article was written by S. E. Haydon, a resident of Aurora. Haydon claimed that the pilot of the aircraft was "not of this world," even going as far as to claim that an Army officer near Fort Worth had determined it was a "Martian." It was also reported that hieroglyphic-like words on metal were found in the wreckage.

Though it occurred 50 years beforehand, many people have compared the Aurora UFO incident to Roswell.

Although supernatural believers want to believe an alien did, in fact, die in Texas, others aren't so sure this is really the case. Many people believe the Aurora UFO incident was a hoax, including former mayor Barbara Brammer.

According to Brammer, the town had gone through a number of devastations during the months leading up to the incident. The local cotton crop had been destroyed, a tragic fire destroyed businesses, a spotted fever caused many fatalities, and a train never made it to town as planned. She believed that the incident was all a hoax to draw people to town.

In 1979, *Time* magazine conducted an interview with an 89-year-old woman, who was a resident at the time of the accident. The woman, who was named Etta Pegues, claimed that S. E. Haydon wrote the article as a joke and to "bring interest to Aurora." Pegues also claimed that there was no windmill on the farm where the accident allegedly occurred.

The Aurora UFO incident was featured in a 2005 episode of *UFO Files*. Two eyewitnesses of the town were interviewed. Though one did see smoke from the crash and both claimed their parents saw the wreckage, neither of the eyewitnesses saw the wreckage themselves. A grave marker with a UFO was found at the Aurora Cemetery, but the cemetery did not grant investigators access to the remains.

UFO Hunters also investigated the incident in a 2008 episode. While the investigators failed to find anything definitive at the cemetery, they were given access to the site of the crash. They did not find anything indicative of the accident. However, they did find evidence of a windmill on the property, which was contradictory to what Pegues said during the *Time* magazine interview.

Did an alien die in this small town in Texas? Did a UFO even crash here at all or was it all for attention?

Whether the Aurora UFO incident was true or merely a hoax, there has been no shortage of other reports of UFO sightings in Texas.

A Texas UFO tracking website claims that there were many sightings in 2017 alone. According to *Community Impact Newspaper*, the highest number of sightings in 2017 were reported in Central Texas.

In 2017, there were nine reports of UFO sightings in Austin and ten more in San Antonio. There was a total of 27 alien sightings reported in all of Central Texas in 2017 alone. These numbers originated from the National UFO Reporting Center.

If you're worried about an alien crashing in your backyard in Texas, try not to worry *too* much. The National UFO Reporting Center says that the number of reported UFO sightings in Texas is actually pretty low, given how geographically large the state is. You'd have to worry more in states like Pennsylvania, New York, Washington, California, and Ohio, which have the highest number of reported sightings.

The Fort Worth Zoo Is Believed to Be Haunted

Lions and tigers and *ghosts*? Oh, my! Many people have claimed to have experienced paranormal encounters at the Fort Worth Zoo. In fact, there are believed to be not just one, but *two* ghosts haunting the zoo.

The first ghost is believed to be that of Michael A. Bell. Bell was a former elephant trainer until his death in 1987. He was tragically crushed when he tried to move several elephants into a larger pen. Since his death, a number of zoogoers have reported seeing a man near the elephant and zebra area of the zoo, the same area the trainer was typically seen when he was alive.

If you're near the zoo café, you might spot another ghost. This one is a woman from the 19th century who is dressed all in white and carries a parasol. People have seen her slowly pacing in front of the café. No one knows what her identity might be, but people claim to see her often. In fact, she apparently looks so lifelike that people have reportedly mistaken her for a zoo employee or actress!

If you take any photos at the Fort Worth Zoo, you might want to see if you notice anything besides the animals.

The Mystery of Ripley's Believe it or Not! And Madame Tussaud's Palace of Wax

If you visit the Ripley's Believe it or Not and Madame Tussaud's Palace of Wax in Grand Prairie, you might not know about the mystery that surrounds it.

Over 30 years ago, there was a fire at the museum that caused 300 wax figures to melt. At the time, the wax collection was the largest in the country and was valued at $4 million. Bob Cox, one of the museum co-owners, claimed that "hobos seeking shelter" had set the fire, according to *D Magazine*.

It was believed that Bob Cox set the fire himself in order to collect insurance money. Cox, who had a long history of financial and gambling problems, was set to go to trial for arson. Patsy Wright, his ex-wife and former co-owner of the museum, was slated to testify against him. However, Wright died 10 days before the trial, which was scheduled to begin in

November of 1987.

On the night of her death, Patsy Wright took Nyquil to fall asleep, as she so often did. But this time, someone had put a lethal dose of strychnine in her Nyquil.

When investigators tried to uncover who had poisoned Wright, they came up with a number of possible theories. However, the most obvious was that Cox had killed her so she couldn't testify against him.

To make things even stranger, a former receptionist at the museum had died unexpectedly in the early '80s. Lori Williams was just 26 years old when she suddenly fell ill and died 11 days later. A cause of death was never determined. She had told a friend that she believed her husband had been poisoning her but is it possible that Cox may have been behind her death as well?

The case appeared on an episode of *Unsolved Mysteries*, and not much has changed. Wright's murder remains an unsolved mystery to date.

Texas Has One of America's Most Haunted Hotels

Do you want to have a sleepover with some spirits? If so, then you might want to take a trip to Austin. The Driskill Hotel in Austin is believed to be one of the most haunted hotels in the entire United States! In fact, the hotel is so well-known for being haunted that the hit song "Ghost of a Texas Ladies Man", by Concrete Blonde, was written about it.

The grand staircase of the hotel is said to be haunted. In 1877, a girl who was chasing a ball accidentally fell down the stairs and died. People have reported hearing giggles and the sound of a ball bouncing on the stairs.

Some have also said that the hotel's founder, Colonel Jesse Driskill, has been known to haunt the place. Driskill was known for smoking cigars and workers have reported randomly smelling cigar smoke. Creepy, right? Well, it gets worse.

It's Room 525 that has been said to be most haunted. Two brides who were on their honeymoon both killed themselves in the bathtub of Room 525. These incidents allegedly took place twenty years apart. The "suicide brides" are said to haunt the room, causing flickering lights, random noises, knocking, and other disturbances that have seriously creeped out guests. Some have even claimed to see apparitions.

Are you still wondering if it's haunted? The best way to find out is to stay there for yourself.

A Stretch of Highway in Texas Was Known to Be Used as A Dumping Ground for Dead Bodies

There's a stretch of highway on I-45 South between the cities of Galveston and Houston where many bodies have been dumped. The highway has been nicknamed the "Highway of Hell." Others were found on a 25-acre patch of land, which is now known as "The Killing Fields."

It's been estimated that about 30 bodies have been found in the area since the 1970s, with the most recent body being discovered in 2016. That being said, it is believed that there are many bodies still out there that haven't yet been found.

Why are so many bodies found in the area? It's been considered the perfect area to get away with murder. The area is so remote that it's said you wouldn't be able to hear someone yelling and that there would be nowhere to run.

So, who's responsible for these deaths? It has long been believed that serial killers are responsible for the majority of these homicides. A lot of the victims shared similar physical features and most of the victims were between the ages of 10 and 25.

There have been several suspects over the years, including a few who have been convicted of some of the murders.

In 1998, a convicted murderer named Edward Harold Bell told police that he was responsible for 11 of the murders. Unfortunately, there wasn't enough evidence to convict him.

A second man was convicted of three of the murders. He's also a suspect, but hasn't been charged, for the murder a fourth victim, whose remains he led police to in 2015 when he was already serving 60 years for kidnapping charges.

A man named Kevin Edison Smith was convicted of murdering Krystal Jean Baker 16 years after her death. He has been sentenced to life in prison.

The majority of the murders are still considered unsolved today.

A movie called *Texas Killing Fields* was released in 2011. The movie is loosely based on the homicides. Although it caused a lot of controversies, particularly with the victims' families, the purpose of the film was to try to raise awareness about the murders and to encourage anyone who may have any information to come forward.

There Are Ghost Towns in Texas

If you're a ghost hunter, the sad news is we're not talking about towns that are haunted by dead people. But what could be eerier than an old abandoned town? If you've seen the movie *The Hills Have Eyes*, then you know just how creepy ghost towns can be!

If you want to explore some ghost towns, then you've come to the right state. Texas is home to 13 ghost towns. Which towns are worth exploring?

The two most well-known ghost towns in Texas are Terlingua and Lobo, which were mining and agricultural towns respectively. Both towns were abandoned when the cost of minerals and agriculture became too expensive after World War II.

Glenrio is another one of Texas's most popular ghost towns. The town, which is located along Route 66, was once hopping. By 1985, however, the town was abandoned. The movie *The Grapes of Wrath* was filmed in Glenrio.

Indianola was once expected to be a beach hotspot that would compete with Galveston. That all changed when two hurricanes hit the town in 1875 and 1886, causing destruction that led the town's residents abandonment of it.

Many of these ghost towns are worth seeing, especially if you've never been to a ghost town before.

Chupacabra Sightings Have Been Reported in Texas

Just mentioning the legendary chupacabra is enough to send farmers running to check their livestock and to spark a heated debate. Some people believe in it, while others aren't so sure. Whether it's real or merely folklore, there have been reports of chupacabra sightings in Texas.

What is a chupacabra, exactly? The animal, which is believed to only exist in folklore, was first reported in Puerto Rico. As a result, the creature's name has Spanish origins. The Spanish translation of "chupar" and "cabra" is "goat-sucker." The chupacabra was known to exist off the blood it drank from livestock, particularly goats.

In 2007, a woman named Phylis Canion spotted a bony, hairless creature with a canine-like body and bluish gray skin on her farm in Cuero, Texas. Later, she began to find that her chickens' necks had been torn open and that they had been drained of their blood. When a neighbor found the creature dead on his property, Canion brought it home. Since then, she and her husband have done numerous documentaries on the creature for networks like *National Geographic*, *Animal Planet*, *Discovery Channel*, and *History Channel*.

The weirdest part about it all was that this wasn't the first report of a chupacabra in Texas. There have been numerous reports of sightings, mostly in Eastern Texas. Ben Redford, a researcher for the Center of Skeptical Inquiry and author of the book *Tracking the Chupacabra*, has even called the Lone Star State a "factory" for the legendary creature.

RANDOM FACTS

1. Five Texas towns made NeighborhoodScout's list of 100 most dangerous cities in America in 2017. The towns, from least to most dangerous, were Beaumont, Lubbock, Houston, Balch Springs, and Odessa.

2. A 19-year-old man in Galveston who bit a woman's neck claimed to be a 500-year-old vampire in 2011. When he was taken to jail, he begged police officers to restrain him out of fear of killing them because he needed to "feed."

3. The USS Lexington, which is located in Corpus Christi, is said to be one of the most haunted ships in the United States. People have claimed to feel the presence of spirits. It's thought that Charly, a former crew member, now haunts the ship and acts as a tour guide. There have also been reports of hearing the sound of screams, cries, and even the distant sound of weapons being fired. The USS Lexington has even been featured on the show *Ghost Hunters*.

4. In 1998, Texas got rid of the "last meal" it once offered to death row inmates. Inmates can blame it all on a man named Lawrence Brewer, who ordered a five-course meal that he later refused

to eat. Some of the foods that Lawrence ordered included a triple bacon cheeseburger, two chicken-fried steaks, a meat lover's pizza, three fajitas, and a pound of barbeque. Now instead of the last meal, a death row inmate's final dish consists of the same items as the other inmates.

5. In a graveyard outside of Anson, Texas, it's said that if you park your car a certain way and flash your headlights three times on a clear night, a strange white light will slowly drift down the road towards your car. The local legend says that the light is actually a woman who's searching for her lost sons. When they were sent to the woods one night, they were told to flash their lantern three times. By the time she got to them, they had been killed. When car headlights flash, it's thought that the woman flashes her lantern back in search of her lost children.

6. Despite the town's name, a murder has never been reported in Slaughter, Texas!

7. A goat was once elected as town mayor in Lajitas, Texas. The goat, whose name is Clay Henry, was elected in 1986. However, he may have had a drinking problem. Clay Henry loved to drink beer.

8. There were sightings of strange lights in Lubbock, Texas, in 1951. There were 20 to 30 flashing lights.

The lights were as bright as stars but much larger. Some spectators thought the lights were UFOs. The US Air Force said the lights were "an easily explainable natural phenomenon," but they never explained what that phenomenon was.

9. The bowie knife is named after the Alamo hero Jim Bowie (1796-1836). His brother, Rezin, designed the hefty weapon.

10. A man reported seeing Big Foot in Kountze, Texas, in 1977. He was having car trouble at night and saw a thin, dark figure that was covered in hair crossing the road near Old Hardin Cemetery.

11. If you do have the good (or bad) luck of seeing Big Foot, it is legal to kill him in Texas.

12. What was believed to be a sea creature washed upon the shore of Texas City during Hurricane Harvey. The long creature that washed ashore had some really frightening-looking teeth. Fortunately, the mystery has been solved! A Museum of Natural History biologist and eel expert determined that the "sea creature" was actually a fangtooth snake-eel.

13. Ghost Road, or the "Light of Saratoga," is a strange phenomenon in Texas. It's a light that randomly appears and disappears at the end of Bragg Road in Hardin County. Though it's often

attributed to swamp gas, there's a local legend that says a railroad worker was decapitated in a railroad accident and the light is his ghost's lantern lighting the way as he searches for his own head.

14. There have been reports of sightings of skin-walkers, or Navajo, who use magic to turn themselves into animals or other disguises. Most of these reports come from South Texas.

15. Marfa, Texas, is home to a strange phenomenon. The Marfa Lights are white to yellow lights that appear and disappear in the sky and then travel to another area of the sky. They happen at any time of the day and during any month of the year. Legends have attributed them to everything from UFOs to Native American spirits. Surely, there must be some scientific explanation?

16. Water Wonderland in Odessa, Texas, used to be a lively water park. It was shut down in 1980 after a series of civil lawsuits were filed over injuries at the park. Today, it's filled with graffiti, squatters, and rattlesnakes. Due to the sense of abandonment you'll get from seeing the old water park, it has been listed as one of the creepiest places in Texas.

17. The "Texas Seven" was a group of seven men who escaped from a maximum-security prison

on December 30, 2000. They were in on charges that included murder. After they escaped prison, the men were featured on *America's Most Wanted*. After a tip was received, four of the men were located in an RV park in January of 2001. Two of the remaining men were caught a couple of days later. The seventh man committed suicide before he was found. The six who had been captured alive were given the death sentence for murder.

18. A lake monster is said to reside in Lake Granbury. It's been nicknamed "One Eye." As you can probably guess, the lake monster is said to only have one eye. It's unknown if the lake monster was only born with one eye or if one of its eyes was injured. One Eye is said to resemble the Loch Ness Monster, with a long neck and humped back. To make things creepier, early Spanish settlers and the Native Americans spoke of something "terrible" and "savage" that lurked in the water of the Brazos River, which flows into Lake Granbury.

19. In March of 2017, space debris from what's believed to be a spacecraft was found in Freeport, Texas.

20. Ever think of freezing your body after you die? As of 2016, the "Mecca of Cryogenics" was being built in Texas. Also nicknamed as the "Center for Immortality," the center is one day expected to

hold 50,000 frozen people who hope to return from the dead.

Test Yourself – Questions and Answers

1. What was the name of the girl whose disappearance led to the AMBER Alerts system?

   a. Amber Hagerman
   b. Amber Portwood
   c. Amber Rose

2. Which Texas man's death led to a law that was signed into legislation to fight against hate crimes?

   a. Matthew Shephard
   b. James Byrd, Jr.
   c. Michael Scott

3. What is the name of the patch of land where dead bodies have been found near I-45?

   a. The Killing Fields
   b. The Highway of Hell
   c. The Patch of Death

4. Which Texas hotel is one of the most haunted hotels in the United States?

   a. Stockyards Hotel
   b. Omni Austin Hotel Downtown
   c. The Driskill Hotel

5. Which Texas city ranks highest in the top 100 dangerous cities in America?

    a. Houston
    b. Beaumont
    c. Odessa

Answers

1. a.
2. b.
3. a.
4. c.
5. c.

CHAPTER SIX

TEXAS'S WILDLIFE, SCIENCE, AND OTHER COOL FACTS!

Have you ever wondered what types of weird animals you might see in Texas? Do you know which animal population was intentionally reduced in Texas? Have you ever wondered if Texas is hurting or helping our environment? You'll find the answers to these and other questions in this chapter!

Texas Hosts the Largest Rattlesnake Round-up in the USA

Texas hosts the largest and oldest rattlesnake round-up in the country.

The first Rattlesnake Round-Up was held in Sweetwater, Texas, in 1958. The purpose of the event was to kill as many rattlesnakes as possible in order to help lower the number of rattlesnakes in the town and surrounding areas.

The Rattlesnake Round-Up has been held in

Sweetwater every year since. However, what was once meant to help a small town has now become an event that draws people from all over!

According to the *San Angelo Standard-Times*, the round-up saw a record-breaking 24,626 pounds of rattlesnakes in 2016. In 2017, more than 8,000 pounds of rattlesnake were killed at the event and over 40,000 people were in attendance. The event consists of a cook-off, a pageant, and more. It also brings more than a whopping $8 million to the local economy.

The round-up has a process they follow when they kill the snakes. They record the weights and genders of the snakes before skinning, beheading, and milking the snakes of their venom. The venom gets made into anti-venom and is sold to pharmaceutical companies. The rattlesnake meat is then deep-fried and served at the festival.

If you have a fear of snakes, we don't recommend attending this event. Just looking at photos from the Rattlesnake Round-Up are enough to give you the heebie-jeebies.

You Can See Dinosaur Tracks in Texas

Have you ever wanted to see some real-life dinosaur tracks? Well, you can in Texas.

Glen Rose, Texas, is considered "The Dinosaur Capital of Texas." Some even consider it to be the

"Dinosaur Capital of the World," although others disagree. Regardless of its title, there's no doubt that this Texas town is a hotspot for those with a love for paleontology.

The first dinosaur tracks were discovered in Glen Rose in 1908 after a flood occurred. It was on the limestone floor of the Paluxy River that the tracks were spotted. Another one of the tracks was also found embedded in the bandstand of the Glen Rose town square, where it can still be found today.

The tracks were made up of large footprints with three toes. It's believed that the tracks belonged to the *Acrocanthosaurus*, which was slightly smaller but similar in shape to a *Tyrannosaurus Rex*.

Later in 1934, more dinosaur prints were discovered. These were larger. Although they were originally mistaken as Woolly Mammoth tracks, the prints are believed to have belonged to Sauropods. Later, a paleontologist discovered sauropod prints the size of small bathtubs!

Today, you can visit Dinosaur Valley State Park, which is located a few miles west of Glen Rose. The park spans 1,500 acres of land and has exhibits of some of the best dinosaur footprints in the entire world. It also exhibits the most well-preserved sauropod footprints that can be found *anywhere*.

As you can imagine, Dinosaur Valley State Park is a

huge tourist spot. It's something you won't want to miss out on if you ever visit Texas. The park offers camping, bike riding, and other activities to visitors.

Texas's Bats Add Value to the State's Economy

If you love bats, then you might want to head to Texas. More species of bats can be found in Texas than any other state in the country. While 27 species of bats can be found in the state, it's rare to see them all.

The most common species in the state are the Mexican free-tailed bat. There's such a high population throughout the state that Texas even recognizes the Mexican free-tailed bat as its state flying mammal. Another one of the most common species of bats in the Lone Star State is the Brazilian free-tailed bat.

The evening bat and big brown bats can be found in East and Southeast Texas forests and woodlands. The red bat can also be found in these areas.

Bracken Cave, which is located in Comal County, Texas, houses the largest bat colony in the entire world! From the months of March to October, somewhere between 20-40 million Mexican free-tailed bats call the cave their home.

The South Congress Bridge in Austin also provides sanctuary to the largest urban bat colony. Austin isn't the only city in Texas where you'll see lots of bats, though. Thousands of bats take refuge under the Waugh Drive Bridge in Houston.

Although they may be creepy to some, bats are actually thought to be extremely useful to Texas farmers. The high population of bats helps to keep the pests that could potentially destroy farms under control.

You might be surprised to learn that bats also offer an economic advantage to the state. Guano, also known as bat poop, is rich in nitrogen and phosphorous. Guano makes a powerful plant fertilizer, and it's also used to make gunpowder.

The mineral is so useful, that in the late 19th century, the U.S. government offered free land to any farmers who found guano reserves and shared them with other American citizens.

Before Texas's oil reserves were discovered, guano was the No. 1 mineral exported by the state.

The bat colony in Bracken Cave produces an estimated 85-100 tons of guano every year. It's estimated that the bat's droppings are nearly 60 feet deep in the cave. They have accumulated there for thousands of years.

So, how is guano extracted from the cave, you wonder? Workers shovel the guano into a hopper, which is attached to a pipe that acts as a vacuum. An industrial vacuum is also used to remove guano from any hard-to-reach areas of the cave.

Over the course of 21 days, it's estimated that about 184,000 pounds, or 4,200 bags, of guano are removed from Bracken Cave.

It's not the safest practice since the ammonia fumes from guano can be dangerous to humans. Workers are required to wear gas masks when they enter the cave to remove the guano.

Unfortunately, Texas's bats are currently at risk. With the discovery of a deadly fungus called white-nose syndrome threatening to destroy America's bat population, scientists are worried that bats—and guano—may be in grave danger.

The United States' Deadliest Disaster Happened in Texas

There is no doubt that Texas is known for its natural disasters, but did you know that the deadliest disaster to *ever* hit the United States took place in Galveston, Texas?

The Great Galveston Hurricane, which is known to locals as the Great Storm of 1900, took place on the island of Galveston on September 8th, 1900. The hurricane was a Category 4 with 145 mph windfalls.

The death toll estimates range between 6,000-12,000,

with most reports claiming there were 8,000 casualties. For comparison's sake, 1,800 people died during Hurricane Katrina. The number of fatalities during Hurricane Harvey was estimated to be around 88.

To put things into perspective, there were so many deaths during the great Galveston Hurricane that it was impossible to bury them all. Many of the dead bodies were dumped at sea. When bodies washed back to shore, many of them were burned in funeral pyres on the beaches.

The high death toll in Galveston can be blamed on several factors. For starters, weather officials didn't take the storm seriously. They thought Galveston had already experienced so many storms that the 1900 hurricane wouldn't be a big deal. Additionally, the storm caused major damage to the city and railways, which meant there was a shortage of food and water.

After the storm, the city of Galveston went through major changes to prevent another hurricane from causing so much damage. The Galveston Seawall was built for protection and the city was elevated by as much as 17 feet using dredged sand.

The Great Galveston Hurricane was the second-costliest hurricane to date. The amount of money spent rebuilding the city was estimated to be around $20 million in 1900, which is the equivalent of $516 million as of 2009. The only hurricane that was costlier than the 1900 Galveston Hurricane was Hurricane Katrina.

Prior to the hurricane, Galveston was the second-richest city in the United States, second only to Newport, RI.

One of America's Most Dangerous Diving Spots is in Texas

Are you a thrill seeker who's always on the lookout for new risks to take? Well, look no further. Jacob's Well is known as one of America's most dangerous diving spots. Though it's hard to find the exact number of people who have died there, it's estimated that the number is about a dozen.

Located near Wimberley, Jacob's Well appears to be safe on the surface. It looks like nothing more than a safe swimming hole. It's what lies *beneath* the surface that's dangerous. There are tight, curved caves underneath the water. Divers have gotten stuck in the caves and suffocated to death.

Despite the numerous deaths that have taken place at Jacob's Well, it's still a popular spot for adventure seekers. In fact, people have traveled from all over to dive at this swimming hole. But it's not for the fainthearted and we wouldn't recommend diving there.

Apparently, even professional divers have died at Jacob's Well. Scuba divers have found it difficult to make it through some of the tight openings with their tanks, having to take them off in order to pass through.

There's no need to avoid Jacob's Well completely! Though it's not a safe place to go diving, it is considered a safe spot for swimmers.

All Astronauts Start Their Training in Texas

One of the biggest tourist spots in all of Texas is the Space Center Houston, which is located in the NASA Johnson Space Center in Houston. You may remember that many movies were filmed at the Johnson Space Center, but did you know that astronauts actually go there for training?

In fact, the Space Center is the first place where *all* astronauts go for their training. Over the past 40 years, more than 3,000 people have begun training for their careers at Space Center Houston.

Space Center Houston is also home to the most popular vacation and summer space camps for kids. People book up to *years* in advance to ensure that their children will have a spot!

So, what can you expect as a tourist to the Space Center? Well, for starters, you'll have to take the NASA Tram Tour before you'll be able to enter the space center. Since the Space Center keeps the facility at 60 degrees regardless of the time of year, you'll want to pack a sweater or jacket.

Some of the most exciting things you can experience as a tourist at the Space Center include a tour of the Saturn V at Rocket Park, an interactive exhibit of Mars, and lunch with a NASA astronaut. That being said, there are so many exhibits and artifacts to be seen here that any NASA fan will be sure to enjoy.

The Largest Ranch in the Country is Located in Texas

Texas is known for its ranches, so it may come as no surprise that the largest ranch in the United States can be found in the Lone Star State. However, it might surprise you to learn just *how* big it is.

King Ranch is set on more than 800,000 acres, making it larger than the state of Rhode Island. According to *The New York Times*, 982 Central Parks could fit inside King Ranch. It's the second-largest ranch in the entire world, second only to Alexandria Station in South Australia!

The ranch was founded by Captain Richard King in 1853. The property was full of creeks and situated in the Wild Horse Desert of South Texas. Located in South Texas, King Ranch spreads into six different counties.

Since it was started, King Ranch has hosted some of the first cattle drives, developed two breeds of cattle (Santa Cruz and Santa Gertrudis), and has bred champion Thoroughbreds and fine Quarter Horses.

King Ranch has long been viewed as a symbol of Texas's power, wealth, and pride.

Today, King Ranch continues to operate as a ranch. It also farms cotton, citrus, sugar cane, grain, and other agricultural goods. Recreational hunting is also enjoyed on the ranch.

There are a number of books that have been written about the King Ranch. Edna Ferber's *Giant*, which was later turned into a movie, is based on King Ranch.

Lords of the Land by Matt Braun is loosely based on King Ranch.

The fictional ranch in James Michener's *Centennial* is also said to be based on King Ranch.

People Go Trophy Hunting in Texas

If you think you need to travel to Africa to go trophy hunting, you'd be wrong. All you need to do is head over to the Lone Star State!

It's surprising for some to know that trophy hunting is a common practice in the United States. Trophy hunting, as a whole, has been extremely controversial, especially since the death of Cecil the Lion in Zimbabwe. However, there are around 1,000 trophy-hunting facilities in the United States and 50% of them are in Texas.

A little-known fact about trophy hunting is that the money spent on trophies goes to protect endangered species. In fact, ranch owners say that certain species would be extinct entirely if it weren't for trophy hunting!

So, what types of animals can you go hunting for in Texas? What types of prices can you expect to pay? Prices vary according to the ranch. Some ranches may offer packages in which they'll transport you to the hunting areas and may even supply you with alcoholic beverages after your hunt.

Zebras are the most popular animal people go to Texas to hunt. The price for a zebra starts around $5,750. You can hunt the nearly-extinct scimitar-horned oryx for prices ranging anywhere from $2,000-$19,000. Wildebeest, antelope, and axis deer are just a few of other types of exotic species that you can hunt if you're willing.

You're probably wondering when this happened. Since when does Texas have exotic animals? It all started back in 1930 when a herd of antelopes arrived on King Ranch. 1988 estimates showed that there were 67 exotic species residing in Texas with 90,400 kept at ranches and more than 70,000 free-ranging. In 2016, it was believed that those numbers had more than *tripled.*

The majority of the exotic animals in the state are said to be found in the Texas Hill Country region.

Texas is Hurting the Environment

Have you ever thought about what impact Texas has on the environment?

Texas is the United States' leading oil refinery state. As of 2012, it was estimated that the state's oil production accounted for nearly a third of all oil production in the United States.

In fact, if it were its own country, it would be the 6th leading nation in oil production. The state has 10 billion barrels of oil reserves and is home to 27 oil refineries, including Exxon and AT&T, Inc. As of 2015, Texas was producing 3.6 million barrels *a day.* That's a lot of oil!

Since it is the largest oil producer in the country, which also means Texas has the highest carbon dioxide emissions in the country as well. This is bad news since carbon dioxide emissions are one of the problems that currently contribute to climate change.

To make matters even worse, Texas is also the leading producer of cattle in the country. As a result, greenhouse gas emissions, or carbon dioxide, released during the agriculture process is higher in Texas than any other state. Research has also found that the methane released from cow belches is another factor that's contributing to global warming.

Most of Texas's Prairie Dog Population Was Killed Off

When you think of prairie dogs, Texas might come to mind. Years ago, black-tailed prairie dogs ran rampant in Texas. They could be seen just about anywhere in West Texas.

Prairie dogs live in colonies called "prairie dog towns." According to *Texas Monthly*, the largest prairie dog town to have existed in Texas was made up of 400 million prairie dogs—or half of the entire rat population living in Manhattan!

While they may look cute at the zoo, prairie dogs have long been considered a pest. The millions of prairie dogs that were living in Texas caused so much destruction to the crops and grass in the state, that it infuriated farmers and ranchers. As a result, they began to poison the prairie dogs in an attempt to get rid of as many of them as possible. Now, it's been estimated by the Texas Parks & Wildlife Foundation that only about one percent of the former prairie dog population remains in the state.

If you want to see some prairie dogs while you're in

Texas, don't fret. The critters can still be seen in the Lone Star State. Efforts have been made to try to preserve the prairie dog, and they can be seen at local zoos.

One of the best places to see prairie dogs in Texas is at Prairie Dog Town in Mackenzie Park in Lubbock. The prairie dog colony was established in 1935 by K. N. Clapp. Clapp feared that the government's poisoning program would lead to the extinction of the prairie dog. He and a friend trapped two pairs of prairie dogs in the park, hoping that they would breed with one another. His vision turned out to be successful. The prairie dogs began to breed and many can be seen there today. In fact, Prairie Dog Town is a tourist hotspot.

Texas is a Really Windy State

Did you know that Texas has more wind farms than any other state in the country? As of 2017, wind energy was the second most popular form of electric in the state. Wind energy is even more common than coal-powered energy in Texas.

Not that this should come as any shock. Texas is known to be a windy state. Corpus Christi, in particular, has received a lot of attention for its high-wind speeds. Its windiness makes it one of the best cities in all of North America for sailing, kiteboarding, windsurfing, and kite flying. Corpus Christi has been host to the Windsurfing World Championships.

You Might Spot a Rare Wild Cat in Texas

There's a pretty good chance of seeing a wild cat in the Lone Star State. The bobcat is frequently spotted throughout the state, but some of the other wild cats tend to be much rarer. That being said, there are still many reports of seeing these cats.

The mountain lion, which is otherwise known as a cougar or puma, used to be found throughout the entire state of Texas. However, this has changed because mountain lions tend to avoid areas with large populations of people. The influx of urbanization caused mountain lions to be driven out of the habitats they once lived in. Nowadays, cougars are generally only found in the mountains of the Trans-Pecos area and in the brushland area of the Rio Grande Plain.

The jaguar is believed to be extinct in Texas. It's believed that the last jaguar in the state was shot and killed in 1946 in San Benito. In 2016, it was said that the last jaguar in the entire United States was living in Arizona. However, this doesn't stop people from reporting sightings of the elusive animal. Could some of them still be out there somewhere?

It's believed that some jaguar sightings might actually be sightings of the ocelot, or leopard cat, due to the similarities in their markings. Others argue that it would be nearly impossible to mistake the two, given the difference in their sizes. While the jaguar weighs between 120 and 210 pounds, the ocelot only weighs between 18 and 44 pounds.

Still, the ocelot *is* out there. Though the ocelot is endangered and facing near extinction, it was estimated in 2017 that there were about 80 ocelots remaining in the Lone Star State. They are found mostly along the state border.

The jaguarundi is another type of wild cat that you might spot in the state. The cat can be identified by its long body, long tail, short legs, and rounded ears. The jaguarundi can be a number of different colors, ranging from blackish and gray/brown to the color of a fox to chestnut colored.

Jaguarundi are also considered rare and are usually spotted in South Texas. Though they are currently on the list of endangered species, the U.S. Fish and Wildlife Service has hopes of increasing the population to 500 by 2050. The jaguarundi is endangered due to loss of habitat caused by urbanization, so the Fish and Wildlife Service's goal is to reintroduce the wild cat to its native Rio Grande Valley.

The Second Largest Canyon is in Texas

The largest canyon in the United States is, without argument, the Grand Canyon. The second-largest canyon in the country is located not too far from Amarillo, Texas.

The Palo Duro Canyon spans 120 miles through the Panhandle. It's anywhere from 6-20 miles wide and reaches depths of more than 800 feet.

The Palo Duro Canyon State Park is the second-largest state park in the country. Visitors can go hiking, biking, and horseback riding across 30 miles of the canyon. While you can camp at the state park, many people choose to stay in the stone and timber cabins.

The New York Times has called the Palo Duro Canyon "the other Grand Canyon." However, there's a world of difference between the two canyons. The Palo Duro Canyon is known for its trees. In fact, the Spanish meaning of "Palo Duro" is "hardwood."

Some of the animals that can be regularly found in the canyon include mule deer, roadrunners, coyotes, and bobcats. It's also home to the endangered Texas horned lizard, as well as other types of lizards and snakes.

The Palo Duro Canyon has a long history. The Comanche Indian tribe sought refuge in the Palo

Duro Canyon. It was one of the last places they lived before being forced onto Oklahoman reservations. In fact, one of the most brutal battles of the Red River War took place in the canyon, during which the United States Army shot more than 1,000 horses in an unexpected attack against the Comanche Indians. Not too long after, the Palo Duro Canyon became the first commercial cattle ranch in history. The state park was established in 1934.

The canyon inspired Georgia O'Keefe's oil painting, "Red Landscape," which you can view at the Plains Panhandle Historical Museum.

Texas Has Two Official State Animals

The armadillo is Texas's official small mammal. The nine-banded armadillo, which is the only species of armadillo that can be found in the United States, was chosen to represent the state in 1995. A distant cousin of the sloth, armadillos coincidentally chose to migrate to Texas around the same time it became a state!

According to State Symbols USA, the armadillo has traits that are representative of true Texas, such as "a deep respect and need for the land, the ability to change and adapt, and a fierce undying love for freedom."

The Longhorn is Texas's official state large mammal.

The animal was chosen due to its history in Texas. It was estimated that 10 million Longhorns were herded into Texas following the Civil War.

Longhorns neared extinction in Texas in the 1920s, but thanks to efforts made by the Texas Forest Service to preserve them in state parks, the animal still exists in the state today.

Before the Longhorn was chosen as Texas's official large mammal, it was already being used as a logo for businesses all throughout Texas.

El Paso is Nicknamed "Sun City"

El Paso is nicknamed "Sun City" because—you guessed it—it's really sunny there! In fact, according to the National Weather Service, El Paso is sunny 302 days a year or 83% of daytime hours. Although it's not the sunniest city in America, it's sunny enough to earn its nickname.

There are a number of events that take place in the city that involve its nickname. For example, El Paso hosts the Sun Bowl each year. It also hosts the Sun City Music Festival and the Sun City Craft Beer Fest.

RANDOM FACTS

1. Texas has more whitetail deer than any other state in the country. In 2017, it was estimated that there were about 3.6 million deer in the state. In addition, Texas is also known to produce the largest whitetail deer in the United States. This is because of the protein in the shrubbery that's eaten by the deer in the Lone Star State.

2. There is a town called Earth, Texas. It's the only town in the world that shares a name with the planet we live on. It's unknown how the town got its name.

3. Texans have been known to eat armadillos. Barbequed armadillos and armadillo chili are two popular foods that can be found at festivals throughout the state. But you might want to think twice before eating it! Research has found that handling armadillos and armadillo consumption are both linked to leprosy. Texas ships its armadillos to research facilities that study the animals to find a cure for the disease.

4. One of the worst droughts to have ever been recorded in American history took place in Texas. The drought has been called one of the "worst natural disasters in history." The majority

of the counties in the state were declared disaster areas. The drought lasted for seven years, beginning in 1950 and ending in 1957. The drought caused the crops to die and led to an overabundance of dust, which got into people's homes. Farmers were forced to feed their cattle prickly pear cactuses. Though droughts in the state have been called worse than the Texas drought of the 1950s, none have lasted as long.

5. Dallas is the largest city in the country that isn't situated on a body of navigable water.

6. El Paso is located at the intersection of three states, two in the United States and one in Mexico: Texas, New Mexico, and Chihuahua. It's the only major city located in Texas that falls into the Mountain Time Zone.

7. Amarillo, Texas, was named after a certain type of yellow grass that grows there. The city was previously called Oneida.

8. The prickly pear cactus is the official state plant of Texas. The prickly pear fruit, which is known as tuna, is commonly used in Texan cuisine. Texas prickly pear cactus jelly is a popular recipe. Native Americans are attributed for finding pharmaceutical uses of the prickly pear cactus. They believed it could treat everything from sunburn to chest congestion.

9. The Fort Worth Zoo, which was opened in 1909, has been rated as one of the top zoos in the entire country. At the time of its opening, the zoo only had a lion, a coyote, a peacock, two bear cubs, an alligator, and some rabbits. There are 7,000 species that can be found at the zoo today.

10. Texas is the state with the highest number of tornadoes in the entire country. The yearly average is just under 140 tornadoes. Between the years of 1951 and 2011, more than 8,000 tornadoes were recorded.

11. Despite having the highest number of tornadoes in the country, the biggest natural disaster threat to people living in Central Texas is flooding. Not only is Texas located in Tornado Alley, but Central Texas has also earned the nickname of Flood Alley.

12. The world's largest supply of helium can be found within 250 miles of Amarillo. In fact, 90% of the recoverable helium in the world can be found underground in Amarillo. Helium isn't a renewable source and is used in many industries.

13. Caddo Lake is considered to be the only natural lake in Texas! However, the Caddo Lake that is seen today is not the lake that was naturally created. Dams have been built to raise the surface of the original body of water. Texas is home to 15

rivers and 3,700 streams.

14. Even though it's often thought of for its deserts, Texas's deserts make up less than 10% of the state. In fact, Big Bend has the only deserts in the state. The majority of Texas is made up of plains, hills, woods, and coastal swamp.

15. It might sound like something straight out of a dystopian movie, but Houston has an underground tunnel system. Located 20 feet below ground, the tunnel runs for 7 miles and spans across 95 blocks. You can find restaurants, stores, and more in Houston's downtown tunnels.

16. The official state shell of Texas is the Lightning Whelk. According to State Symbols USA, the shell was chosen as the state shell due to its beauty, how frequently it is found in the state, and because it's only found along the West Coast of the Gulf of Mexico.

17. Dallas has been called "The Crossroads" because it is considered to be an intersection between Los Angeles, New York, Chicago, and Mexico City.

18. There's a replica of the Stonehenge that has been constructed in Ingram, Texas. Though it's not an archaeological phenomenon like the original, Stonehenge II is still a pretty thing to see.

19. Hamilton Pool, which is located near Austin, is one of the most remarkable sights of nature to be

observed in Texas. It's a natural spring that's situated in limestone bedrock. Its water comes from an underground river. There's a deep overhang in one of the walls of the cavern that's of much interest to visitors. Over 100 years ago, the Hamilton Pool was completely covered by a dome that later collapsed. The Hamilton Pool is one of Texas's many tourist attractions.

20. Texas had the most damaging thunderstorm of all-time. In May of 1995, hailstones bigger than cricket balls fell in Fort Worth and Tarrant County. The hailstones that fell during that storm were up to 4" in diameter. The storm cost a whopping $2 billion in damage and injured about 100 people.

Test Yourself – Questions and Answers

1. What year did the Galveston Hurricane happen?

   a. 1991
   b. 1990
   c. 1900

2. Which town is "The Dinosaur Capital of Texas"?

   a. Glen Gardner
   b. Glen Rose
   c. Austin

3. What are the two state animals of Texas?

   a. Armadillo and zebra
   b. Armadillo and Longhorn
   c. Longhorn and prairie dog

4. What is the name of the only naturally occurring lake in Texas?

   a. Caddo Lake
   b. Texas Lake
   c. Houston Lake

5. What animal is most commonly hunted by trophy hunters in Texas?

   a. Antelope
   b. Wildebeest
   c. Zebras

Answers

1. c.
2. b.
3. b.
4. a.
5. c.

DON'T FORGET YOUR
FREE BOOKS

GET THEM AT WWW.TRIVIABILL.COM

MORE BOOKS BY BILL O'NEILL

I hope you enjoyed this book and learned something new. Please feel free to check out some of my previous books on Amazon.

Made in the USA
Coppell, TX
21 April 2021

54229293R00098